Blogging

POINT COUNTERPOINT

Blogging

David L. Hudson, Jr.

SERIES CONSULTING EDITOR
Alan Marzilli, M.A., J.D.

CHELSEA HOUSE
PUBLISHERS

An imprint of Infobase Publishing

To Gene Policinski: a great defender of the First Amendment and blogging.

Blogging

Copyright © 2008 by Infobase Publishing

All rights reserved. No part of this book may be reproduced or utilized in any form or by any means, electronic or mechanical, including photocopying, recording, or by any information storage or retrieval systems, without permission in writing from the publisher. For information, contact:

Chelsea House
An imprint of Infobase Publishing
132 West 31st Street
New York NY 10001

Library of Congress Cataloging-in-Publication Data

Hudson, David L., 1969-
  Blogging / David L. Hudson.
      p. cm. — (Point/counterpoint)
  Includes bibliographical references and index.
  ISBN-13: 978-0-7910-9645-1 (hardcover : acid-free paper)
  ISBN-10: 0-7910-9645-9 (hardcover : acid-free paper) 1. Blogs. 2. Online journalism. I. Title. II. Series.

  TK5105.8884.H83 2007
  006.7—dc22   2007024345

Chelsea House books are available at special discounts when purchased in bulk quantities for businesses, associations, institutions, or sales promotions. Please call our Special Sales Department in New York at (212) 967-8800 or (800) 322-8755.

You can find Chelsea House on the World Wide Web at
http://www.chelseahouse.com

Series design by Keith Trego
Cover design by Keith Trego and Ben Peterson

Printed in the United States of America

Bang NMSG 10 9 8 7 6 5 4 3

This book is printed on acid-free paper.

All links and Web addresses were checked and verified to be correct at the time of publication. Because of the dynamic nature of the Web, some addresses and links may have changed since publication and may no longer be valid.

CONTENTS

Foreword

Alan Marzilli, M.A., J.D.
Washington, D.C.

The debates presented in POINT/COUNTERPOINT are among the most interesting and controversial in contemporary American society, but studying them is more than an academic activity. They affect every citizen; they are the issues that today's leaders debate and tomorrow's will decide. The reader may one day play a central role in resolving them.

Why study both sides of the debate? It's possible that the reader will not yet have formed any opinion at all on the subject of this volume—but this is unlikely. It is more likely that the reader will already hold an opinion, probably a strong one, and very probably one formed without full exposure to the arguments of the other side. It is rare to hear an argument presented in a balanced way, and it is easy to form an opinion on too little information; these books will help to fill in the informational gaps that can never be avoided. More important, though, is the practical function of the series: Skillful argumentation requires a thorough knowledge of *both* sides—though there are seldom only two, and only by knowing what an opponent is likely to assert can one form an articulate response.

Perhaps more important is that listening to the other side sometimes helps one to see an opponent's arguments in a more human way. For example, Sister Helen Prejean, one of the nation's most visible opponents of capital punishment, has been deeply affected by her interactions with the families of murder victims. Seeing the families' grief and pain, she understands much better why people support the death penalty, and she is able to carry out her advocacy with a greater sensitivity to the needs and beliefs of those who do not agree with her. Her relativism, in turn, lends credibility to her work. Dismissing the other side of the argument as totally without merit can be too easy—it is far more useful to understand the nature of the controversy and the reasons *why* the issue defies resolution.

The most controversial issues of all are often those that center on a constitutional right. The Bill of Rights—the first ten amendments to the U.S. Constitution—spells out some of the most fundamental rights that distinguish the governmental system of the United States from those that allow fewer (or other) freedoms. But the sparsely worded document is open to interpretation, and clauses of only a few words are often at the heart of national debates. The Bill of Rights was meant to protect individual liberties; but the needs of some individuals clash with those of society as a whole, and when this happens someone has to decide where to draw the line. Thus the Constitution becomes a battleground between the rights of individuals to do as they please and the responsibility of the government to protect its citizens. The First Amendment's guarantee of "freedom of speech," for example, leads to a number of difficult questions. Some forms of expression, such as burning an American flag, lead to public outrage—but nevertheless are said to be protected by the First Amendment. Other types of expression that most people find objectionable, such as sexually explicit material involving children, are not protected because they are considered harmful. The question is not only where to draw the line, but how to do this without infringing on the personal liberties on which the United States was built.

The Bill of Rights raises many other questions about individual rights and the societal "good." Is a prayer before a high school football game an "establishment of religion" prohibited by the First Amendment? Does the Second Amendment's promise of "the right to bear arms" include concealed handguns? Is stopping and frisking someone standing on a corner known to be frequented by drug dealers a form of "unreasonable search and seizure" in violation of the Fourth Amendment? Although the nine-member U.S. Supreme Court has the ultimate authority in interpreting the Constitution, its answers do not always satisfy the public. When a group of nine people—sometimes by a five-to-four vote—makes a decision that affects the lives of hundreds of millions, public outcry can be expected. And the composition of the Court does change over time, so even a landmark decision is not guaranteed to stand forever. The limits of constitutional protection are always in flux.

These issues make headlines, divide courts, and decide elections. They are the questions most worthy of national debate, and this series aims to cover them as thoroughly as possible. Each volume sets out some of the key arguments surrounding a particular issue, even some views that most people consider extreme or radical—but presents a balanced perspective on the issue. Excerpts from the relevant laws and judicial opinions and references to central concepts, source material, and advocacy groups help the reader to explore the issues even further and to read "the letter of the law" just as the legislatures and the courts have established it.

It may seem that some debates—such as those over capital punishment and abortion, debates with a strong moral component—will never be resolved. But American history offers numerous examples of controversies that once seemed insurmountable but now are effectively settled, even if only on the surface. Abolitionists met with widespread resistance to their efforts to end slavery, and the controversy over that issue threatened to cleave the nation in two; but today public debate over the merits of slavery would be unthinkable, though racial inequalities still plague the nation. Similarly unthinkable at one time was suffrage for women and minorities, but this is now a matter of course. Distributing information about contraception once was a crime. Societies change, and attitudes change, and new questions of social justice are raised constantly while the old ones fade into irrelevancy.

Whatever the root of the controversy, the books in POINT/ COUNTERPOINT seek to explain to the reader the origins of the debate, the current state of the law, and the arguments on both sides. The goal of the series is to inform the reader about the issues facing not only American politicians, but all of the nation's citizens, and to encourage the reader to become more actively involved in resolving these debates, as a voter, a concerned citizen, a journalist, an activist, or an elected official. Democracy is based on education, and every voice counts—so every opinion must be an informed one.

The Internet has turned more of us into writers. Anyone with access to a computer connected to the Internet can create a "blog" to share personal thoughts or commentary on specific topics with the world. As blogging has exploded in popularity, the practice has created numerous controversies.

Because the Internet drastically reduces the cost of publishing, the number of news sources has increased—or has it? One of the controversies examined in this volume is whether blogs should be considered news sources, with bloggers receiving the same privileges and protections of traditional journalists. Some say that the U.S. Constitution makes no distinction among members of the press and that bloggers have broken important news stories. Detractors, however, point out that bloggers do not have their jobs or their publications' reputations on the line, and therefore they do not uphold the standards of the journalistic profession.

The accessibility of the Internet to the world creates additional controversies. When students are away from school, what they say or write is typically shielded from school authorities. When students create blogs, however, school officials can read them, and they are often shocked by the content. Similarly, employees complain about work all the time, but there is a difference between complaining to one's spouse at the dinner table or commiserating with co-workers at a bar, on the one hand, and creating a blog criticizing one's employer on the other. People disagree as to whether posting information in a blog is a legitimate source of concern for school officials or employers, and courts and legislatures nationwide have addressed these issues, often with differing results.

Blogging

The Internet has been hailed as "the most participatory form of mass speech yet developed" and a "far more speech enhancing medium than print."[1] It allows individuals to become modern-day pamphleteers, to contribute to the marketplace of ideas that for so long has been dominated by a relatively select few.

In the late 1990s, a new medium developed on the Internet, which increased the participatory nature of online expression even more. Blogger Jorn Barger referred to this development as a "weblog." Barger coined this phrase to refer to his Web site, which consisted of a series of links to news articles and other sites he found interesting and informative. Barger formed the term by combining the words "Web site" and "logging"—hence, the word *weblog* is now in our cultural lexicon.[2]

Then, in 1999, Peter Merholz coined the term "blog" to refer to a weblog. He wrote on his site, "I've decided to pronounce the word 'Weblog' as 'weeblog' or 'blog' for short."[3] The word caught on like wildfire, even earning the 2004 Word of the Year from Merriam-Webster, the popular dictionary publisher.[4] It has morphed into a verb—*to blog*—and has also formed part of a larger noun—the *blogosphere*. But many users do not agree on a definition of blogging. Robert A. Cox, president of the Media Bloggers Association, describes the word *blogging* as "terrible."

Blogs have become amazingly popular in a short space of time. There are anywhere between 10 and 30 million blogs in the United States, according to a 2006 study by Technorati. The study indicates there are about 100,000 new blogs created daily.[5] The blogosphere has become nearly as influential as other media for many people in the world.

Blogs are online journals or diaries in which individuals can post entries about the subjects that interest them most. Many bloggers link to other sites that contain interesting articles.

Robert Cox, President of the Media Bloggers Association

The word *blogging* is terrible. It is worse than useless because it is an empty vessel into which people can—and do—pour whatever meaning suits them at the time. This breeds confusion and stands in the way of what I believe is the most important development in the media over the past several years—the growth of what is often referred to as "citizens media" or "grassroots journalism." ... Blogging is writing, period.

Source: Quoted in David L. Hudson, Jr. "Blogs and the First Amendment." First Amendment Center Online, November 2005. http://www.firstamendmentcenter.org/press/topic .aspx?topic=blogging.

According to Jonathan Yang's *Rough Guide to Blogging*, "It's those links between blogs that make the blogosphere such a dynamic, interrelated whole."[6] The blogosphere simply covers every subject imaginable: It is as diverse as human thought. Bloggers write about everything from the appellate courts to their favorite sports teams, from presidential snafus to great chess strategies. There are blogs on music, business, the arts, video games, pets, politics, and more.

Many people have entered the blogosphere with great success. Washington D.C.–based attorney Thomas Goldstein, who practices almost exclusively before the U.S. Supreme Court, created the so-called SCOTUS Blog, which examines legal developments related to the U.S. Supreme Court. It has been a tremendous success for him and his wife, Amy Howe, who is also an attorney. "The blog has certainly been much more successful than we could have imagined," Goldstein said.

> We were very excited to start with a couple of hundred hits a day. Now, even on days when the Court isn't doing anything, we get 10k and we can get up to around 100k on truly huge days. By far, the biggest reason that people know who I am (if they do) is the blog. . . . I thought it would be a good way to occupy some of the space in the niche of S. Ct. practice. We already were watching the Court closely, and I thought we could use that information effectively through a blog.[7]

Issues in Blogging

This book seeks to explore several pressing topics involving the blogosphere. Among these topics is the question of whether bloggers who write about the news and other matters of public interest should qualify for protection under existing and future reporter shield laws. This issue is important because bloggers have broken many news stories throughout the past decade, including, but not limited to the affairs of presidents, mainstream

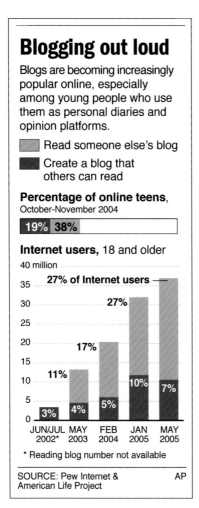

Blogging out loud

Blogs are becoming increasingly popular online, especially among young people who use them as personal diaries and opinion platforms.

▨ Read someone else's blog

■ Create a blog that others can read

Percentage of online teens, October-November 2004

19% | 38%

Internet users, 18 and older

40 million

27% of Internet users —

27%

17%

11%

10%

7%

3% 4% 5%

JUN/JUL 2002* | MAY 2003 | FEB 2004 | JAN 2005 | MAY 2005

* Reading blog number not available

SOURCE: Pew Internet & American Life Project   AP

Blogs have become increasingly popular in recent years for both readers and writers. The immediacy and ad hoc nature of blogs make them especially useful for chronicling daily events, such as a teenager's life or a politician's experiences on the campaign trail. This graphic shows the rise in the popularity of blogs among teens.

media incompetence, and intemperate remarks made by public officials. Without blogs, such stories might not have broken in a time-sensitive manner, or at all. Critics, however, charge that most bloggers are not trained journalists and simply do not place a premium on accuracy. If bloggers continue to make more and more of an impact on consumer consumption of news, the law world will have to take notice of the pressing issue of legal protection for bloggers.

Another issue examined is that of employees who blog and then face repercussions from their employers. This phenomenon has a special name—"doocing" (explained later)—and riles Internet free-speech activists. Many employees have been fired because they have criticized superiors, revealed information about the personal lives of their co-workers, conveyed trade secrets to the public, engaged in illegal conduct, or allowed third-parties to deal in obscenity or other offensive material. The range of conduct is virtually unlimited, but the issue is vitally important for millions of workers. The book deals with both private employees and public employees.

The third major issue examines whether school officials should be allowed to punish public school students for content on the students' blogs. A balance must be drawn between ensuring student and teacher safety while protecting freedom of speech. It is important to realize that the First Amendment does not protect all forms of speech. The First Amendment does not protect perjury, blackmail, false advertising, true threats, incitement to imminent lawless action, and "fighting" words, to name just a few.

Some student speech may cross the line into one of these unprotected categories. Students across the country have been punished for making threats, posting hit lists of other students, assuming false identities of teachers, and writing violently themed material. This issue resonates deeply with many Americans, particularly since Eric Harris, one of the two shooters in the Columbine High School massacre, posted much of his disturbing thinking on his own Web site. His site contained numerous rants, including: "God, I can't wait until I can kill you people." Local neighbors reported that Harris had threatened their son on the Internet.[8]

On the other side of the coin, however, many students have been punished for blogs that are merely critical of school officials. This happens despite the fact that the First Amendment protects both critical and satirical speech. Some school officials have punished students simply for critical speech that they disliked. This raises a looming First Amendment problem.

According to a recently released report on bloggers conducted by the PEW Internet Project, "Blogging is inspiring a new group of writers and creators to share their voices in the world." The report found that 12 million American adults keep a blog and 39 percent of Internet users in the United States—57 million people—read blogs.[9] These numbers mean that the legal and social issues surrounding blogging are not just important to a niche group of computer users and Internet enthusiasts. Blogging and the information contained within blogs reaches tens of millions of people, making it a communication medium that reaches into all corners of the United States and, indeed, the world.

Many Bloggers Are Journalists Who Deserve the Protection of a Reporter Shield Law

Two writers uncover a great deal of state governmental corruption through a confidential source in the state government. This confidential source leaks secrets to these two writers, divulging information about an elaborate scheme of bribes, kick-backs, and other unsavory transactions. This scenario represents some of the highest traditions of a free and vigorous press, which, in its role as the fourth estate, serves as a check upon the three other official branches of government. However, there are significant differences between the two journalists. One works for a mainstream press publication, obtaining credentials at all major public events on his beats. The other is a blogger, a renegade truth-seeker who is a constant thorn in the sides of the power structure.

The state has a reporter shield law that protects journalists from intrusive governmental actions that attempt to turn reporters into handmaidens of the state. Under this state law, in order to compel a journalist to reveal his or her sources, the government must meet a high standard. The government must show that the material sought by the journalist is highly relevant and cannot be obtained by alternative means.

In the scenario above, the press reporter may well be able to escape punishment because of the shield law; however, the state law does not cover bloggers—even bloggers who engage in traditional newsgathering and reporting functions. Many critics believe that bloggers are not entitled to the protections of mainstream journalists. Second- or third-class treatment remains the unfortunate reality for many bloggers.

A major legal issue regarding bloggers and the First Amendment is whether bloggers should be treated as reporters for purposes of a proposed federal reporter-shield law. Is a blogger who reports about a large computer company's products before they are released to the public violating trade secrets, or is he engaging in First Amendment–protected activity? Would the blogger be covered by a state shield law?

Bloggers have made a major contribution to journalism.

Some bloggers have broken stories of great public import. Kurt Opsahl, staff attorney for the Electronic Frontier Foundation and an expert on law relating to bloggers, says there have been many instances in which bloggers expanded on a story the mainstream media had let slip by. One instance was when Senator Trent Lott publicly praised the politics of Senator Strom Thurmond, a supporter of racial segregation in the mid twentieth century. Senator Lott had praised Senator Thurmond at a December 2002 meeting, saying: "When Strom Thurmond ran for president, we voted for him. We're proud of it. And if the rest of the country had followed our lead, we wouldn't have had all these problems over the years, either." To many people, those comments made it sound as though Lott himself was voicing regret over the desegregation of busses, schools, and other public buildings and facilities here. "Bloggers hammered on the Trent Lott story until mainstream media was forced to pick it up again," Opsahl said. Pressure grew and Lott eventually resigned his leadership position in the U.S. Senate.

Bloggers have broken many other major stories. "Three amateur journalists at the Powerline.com blog were primarily responsible for discrediting the documents used in CBS's rush-to-air story on President George Bush's National Guard service. And the list goes on," Opsahl said.[10] Robert Cox, director of the Media Bloggers Association, lists several other national-headline stories affected greatly by blog reporting: Dan Rather and the Texas Air National Guard memos—false documents that called into question President George W. Bush's service in the National Guard during the Vietnam War—and the Swift Boat Veterans for Truth controversy are two examples. (The Swift Boat Veterans were a group formed to oppose 2004 Democratic presidential nominee John Kerry, whom the group alleged had exaggerated his own military record in Vietnam.)

"The influence of blogs on both the traditional mainstream media and the public discourse cannot be overestimated," writes law professor Mary-Rose Papandrea. "Online contributors have broken a number of stories that the mainstream media originally either ignored or downplayed."[11]

Bloggers deserve the protection of shield laws and should be covered by a federal shield law.

For many years, reporters have sought a federal shield law. The push for shield laws intensified after the U.S. Supreme Court refused to recognize a First Amendment–based privilege for journalists seeking an exemption from a grand jury subpoena. The court ruled 5 to 4 in *Branzburg v. Hayes* (1972) that reporters do not have a First Amendment right to avoid testifying before a grand jury as long as the subpoena was issued in good faith.[12] The reporters involved in the case contended that forcing reporters to testify and reveal their confidential sources would burden their future newsgathering efforts. The result, according to the press, would be that potential confidential sources would be far less willing to talk to reporters. This would result in the public receiving less information about important issues.

Justice Byron White reasoned that the press was entitled to no special protections that were not also given to the public, and therefore members of the press were not entitled to exemptions from civic duties such as grand jury testimony. White was partly concerned with how to decide who merited any such privileges. He felt that it would be hard to limit the privilege to those who really might deserve it. He explained:

> We are unwilling to embark the judiciary on a long and difficult journey to such an uncertain destination. The administration of a constitutional newsman's privilege would present practical and conceptual difficulties of a high order. Sooner or later, it would be necessary to define those categories of newsmen who qualified for the privilege, a questionable procedure in light of the traditional doctrine that liberty of the press is the right of the lonely pamphleteer who uses carbon paper or a mimeograph just as much as of the large metropolitan publisher who utilizes the latest photocomposition methods. . . . The informative function asserted by representatives of the organized press in the present cases is also performed by lecturers, political pollsters, novelists, academic researchers, and dramatists. Almost any author may quite accurately assert that he is contributing to the flow of information to the public, that he relies on confidential sources of information, and that these sources will be silenced if he is forced to make disclosures before a grand jury.[13]

White seemingly discounted the fact that the First Amendment does not require distinguishing between "legitimate" and illegitimate publishers. He also seemingly minimized the history of revolutionary pamphleteers who criticized the British government in the Revolutionary War times. Although there is some merit to White's concern, Justice Potter Stewart had the better view in his well-reasoned dissent. He warned that the majority's opinion "invites state and federal authorities to undermine the historic independence of the press by attempting to annex the journalistic profession as an investigative arm of government."[14] For this reason, Stewart posited that before the government could require a reporter to reveal his confidential source and confidentially obtained material, the government must:

> (1) show that there is probable cause to believe that the newsman has information that is clearly relevant to a specific probable violation of law; (2) demonstrate that the information sought cannot be obtained by alternative means less destructive of First Amendment rights; and (3) demonstrate a compelling and overriding interest in the information.[15]

Stewart's dissent provided the blueprint for future shield laws. More than 30 states have enacted reporter shield statutes. In May 2007, the Texas House of Representatives passed a state shield law. Connecticut enacted a shield law in 2006. The rest of the states, except Hawaii, have recognized a similar-type privilege in their common law (common law is judge-made law, as opposed to laws passed by the legislature).

But there is still no federal shield law. This is a problem because there has been an upswing in the number of times that federal prosecutors have sought confidential-source information from reporters. Judith Miller, then a reporter for the *New York Times*, spent more than 80 days in jail in 2005 for refusing to divulge a confidential source. And blogger Josh Wolf, a self-described freelance video journalist, spent 226 days in jail for refusing to turn over his video from a chaotic 2005 San Francisco street protest during the G-8 summit. In addition to refusing to turn over the video, Wolf would not testify as to whether he knew who had torched a police car during the street protest.[16]

Josh Wolf recorded a video of the scene at the San Francisco protest of the 2005 G-8 Summit. When he refused to hand over the tape to law enforcement authorities, he was arrested and jailed for 226 days. Above, Wolf speaks during a press conference after leaving jail on bail on September 1, 2006.

Many journalists—both mainstream journalists and blogger types—rallied to Wolf's cause, believing that the government overreached in punishing him in such an extreme way simply because he refused to testify and turn over his video.[17]

Congress should pass a federal shield law that would define journalism broadly enough to include at least some bloggers.

Bloggers and other journalists need a federal shield law to protect them from federal prosecutors searching for case evidence. Congress is debating several bills that would provide for a federal shield law for reporters. In October 2005, the Senate

Judiciary Committee held a second hearing on such proposed legislation. At the hearing, Senator John Cornyn of Texas said that there needed to be a "serious discussion of what constitutes the term 'reporter.'"

The measure was re-introduced as the Free Flow of Information Act of 2007. At that time, there seemed to be a realization that many bloggers were in fact journalists, because they engaged in journalistic functions such as gathering information and writing analyses. The 2007 proposal appeared to define journalism broadly: "The term 'journalism' means the gathering, preparing, collecting, photographing, recording, writing,

Under Consideration by the Federal Legislature: The Free Flow of Information Act of 2007

The following document excerpt is a proposed bill, not a law.

(a) **Conditions for Compelled Disclosure:** In any proceeding or in connection with any issue arising under Federal law, a Federal entity **may not compel** a covered person to provide testimony or produce any document related to information possessed by such covered person as part of engaging in journalism, unless a court determines by a preponderance of the evidence, after providing notice and an opportunity to be heard to such covered person—

   (1) that the party seeking to compel production of such testimony or document has exhausted all reasonable alternative sources (other than a covered person) of the testimony or document;

   (2) that—

      (A) in a criminal investigation or prosecution, based on information obtained from a person other than the covered person—

         (i) there are reasonable grounds to believe that a crime has occurred; and

         (ii) the testimony or document sought is essential to the investigation or prosecution or to the defense against the prosecution; or

editing, reporting, or publishing of news or information that concerns local, national, or international events or other matters of public interest for dissemination to the public."[18]

Existing state shield laws should be amended to cover bloggers or be read broadly.

The question of whether a blogger is covered by a reporter shield law was answered in the affirmative by the California Court of Appeals in *O'Grady v. The Superior Court of Santa Clara County*.[19] Although the decision only covers the state of California, it could be persuasive to courts nationwide.

(B) in a matter other than a criminal investigation or prosecution, based on information obtained from a person other than the covered person, the testimony or document sought is essential to the successful completion of the matter;

(3) in the case that the testimony or document sought could reveal the identity of a source of information or include any information that could reasonably be expected to lead to the discovery of the identity of such a source, that—

(A) disclosure of the identity of such a source is necessary to prevent imminent and actual harm to national security with the objective to prevent such harm;

(B) disclosure of the identity of such a source is necessary to prevent imminent death or significant bodily harm with the objective to prevent such death or harm, respectively; or

(C) disclosure of the identity of such a source is necessary to identify a person who has disclosed—

(i) a trade secret of significant value in violation of a State or Federal law ...

Source: The Free Flow of Information Act of 2007, S. 1267. The Library of Congress. http://thomas.loc.gov/cgi-bin/query/C?c110:./temp/~c110rPBR1p.

The case involved Jason O'Grady, who ran the online magazine *PowerPage*. On this Web site, O'Grady wrote four articles about future Apple computer products related to the storage of digital music. Apple's attorneys responded quite vehemently, insisting that O'Grady immediately remove the articles because they involved the appropriation of trade secrets. The Apple attorneys claimed the articles harmed the company financially by giving its competitors the opportunity to offer similar products and business strategies. The attorneys sought a subpoena

FROM THE BENCH

California Court of Appeals in *O'Grady v. The Superior Court of Santa Clara County*, 139 Cal. App. 4th 1423 (2006)

We decline the implicit invitation to embroil ourselves in questions of what constitutes "legitimate journalis[m]." The shield law is intended to protect the gathering and dissemination of *news*, and that is what petitioners did here. We can think of no workable test or principle that would distinguish "legitimate" from "illegitimate" news. Any attempt by courts to draw such a distinction would imperil a fundamental purpose of the *First Amendment*, which is to identify the best, most important, and most valuable ideas not by any sociological or economic formula, rule of law, or process of government, but through the rough and tumble competition of the memetic marketplace.

Nor does Apple supply any colorable ground for declaring petitioners' activities not to be legitimate newsgathering and dissemination. Apple asserts that petitioners merely reprinted "verbatim copies" of Apple's internal information while exercising "no editorial oversight at all." But this characterization, if accepted, furnishes no basis for denying petitioners the protection of the statute. A reporter who uncovers newsworthy documents cannot rationally be denied the protection of the law because the publication for which he works chooses to publish facsimiles of the documents rather than editorial summaries. The shield exists not only to protect editors but equally if not more to protect newsgatherers. The primacy Apple would grant to editorial function cannot be justified by any rationale known to us.

ordering O'Grady to reveal the source of his information about Apple's future products.

One of several legal issues in the case concerned whether California's reporter shield law covered O'Grady. California is the rare state that actually provides protection for journalists in its state constitution, as opposed to in a standard statute or law. The provision in the California Constitution provides: "A publisher, editor, reporter, or other person connected with or employed upon a newspaper, magazine, or other periodical

Moreover, an absence of editorial judgment cannot be inferred merely from the fact that some source material is published verbatim. It may once have been unusual to reproduce source materials at length, but that fact appears attributable to the constraints of pre-digital publishing technology, which compelled an editor to decide how to use the limited space afforded by a particular publication. This required decisions not only about what information to include but about how to compress source materials to fit. In short, editors were forced to summarize, paraphrase, and rewrite because there was not room on their pages to do otherwise.

Digital communication and storage, especially when coupled with hypertext linking, make it possible to present readers with an unlimited amount of information in connection with a given subject, story, or report. The only real constraint now is time—the publisher's and the reader's. From the reader's perspective, the ideal presentation probably consists of a top-level summary with the ability to "drill down" to source materials through hypertext links. The decision whether to take this approach, or to present original information at the top level of an article, is itself an occasion for editorial judgment. Courts ought not to cling too fiercely to traditional preconceptions, especially when they may operate to discourage the seemingly salutary practice of providing readers with source materials rather than subjecting them to the editors' own "spin" on a story.

Source: 139 Cal. App. 4th 1423 (2006).

publication . . . shall not be adjudged in contempt . . . for refusing to disclose the source of any information procured" during the newsgathering process.

The appeals court applied the proper analysis to this case, reasoning that many bloggers' sites are functionally equivalent to newspapers, magazines, and other materials in the print world that are classically considered the domains of journalists. The court gave a broad reading to the state statute's terms "magazine" and "other periodical publication," reasoning that O'Grady's Web site fell under these terms, and also determined that much of the posting on a Web site "appears conceptually indistinguishable from publishing a newspaper."[20] The appeals court also rejected the contention that Web sites were somehow different from the print, radio, and television media. According to the court, O'Grady's Web site bears "closer resemblance to traditional print media than do television and radio."[21] The appeals court concluded that the Web site was entitled to the state shield protection.

Gregg Leslie, legal defense director for the Reporters Committee for Freedom of the Press, says that asking whether bloggers are journalists is the wrong question.

> "Bloggers" is a vague, amorphous term like 'telephone users.' . . . Just like some telephone users are journalists and some are not; the same thing with bloggers. The medium doesn't answer the question. It has more to do with the function that the person is performing. That's how we have approached the shield law question. If the bloggers' involvement is to report information to the public and to gather information for that purpose openly then they should be treated like a journalist. . . . There should be a functional analysis in addition to or instead of the current analysis of what medium you are writing in.[22]

Kurt Opsahl, the attorney with Electronic Frontier Foundation, concurred: "As the courts have confirmed, what makes journalism journalism is not the format but the content. Where news is gathered for dissemination to the public, it is journalism—regardless of whether it is printed on paper or distributed through the Internet."[23]

Summary

Some blogs may be nothing more than personal rants that contribute little to the marketplace of ideas. But many blogs fulfill the high purpose of the First Amendment by contributing to the marketplace of ideas. Many standard newspapers now offer their own blogs on their online editions. Some of them link to individual bloggers. Many newspaper reporters now have their own blogs, too. This shows that even the "establishment" recognizes that some blogs are deserving of protection of the journalist privilege. Robert Cox of the Media Bloggers Association explains:

> The Media Bloggers Association accepts the Wikipedia definition of journalism as "a discipline of collecting, verifying, reporting and analyzing information gathered regarding current events, including trends, issues, and people. We believe blogging is not only a publishing medium but a vibrant form of personal expression in which our members slip in and out of roles as journalists, reviewers, poets, pundits, or provocateurs with each post. It is our contention that when our members practice journalism, they have the same rights and responsibilities as any other journalist and must be accorded the same First Amendment rights and legal privileges as those who work for traditional media organizations.[24]

Many of the leaders of colonial America wrote anonymous tracts criticizing the British government. Christopher Daly writes that, "bloggers stand squarely in a long-standing journalistic tradition."[25] At least some bloggers are similar to their Revolutionary War–era counterparts in that both groups are independent, often challenging of governmental regulation or authority, and, most importantly, contribute to the marketplace of ideas.

Daly says it best: "Anyone who engages in reporting—whether for newspapers, magazines, radio, television, or blogs—deserves equal protection under the laws, whether the news is delivered with a quill pen or a computer."[26]

Bloggers Should Not Receive the Protections of Mainstream Journalists

The proliferation of communications media in the modern world makes it impossible to construct a reasonable or useful definition of who would be a "reporter" eligible to claim protection from a newly minted common law privilege. Reporters cannot be readily identified. They do not have special courses of study or special degrees. They are not licensed. They are not subject to any form of organized oversight or discipline.

—U.S. District Judge Rosemary Collyer[27]

John Seigenthaler is a longtime journalist, respected and revered in civil rights and First Amendment circles. He is the founder of the First Amendment Center, and was previously the editor and publisher of *The Tennessean*, a large newspaper based in Nashville, Tennessee. He was also the founding editorial director of the national newspaper *USA Today*. He also served

29

as an assistant to U.S. Attorney General Robert Kennedy in the early 1960s.

Seigenthaler was known for his support of activists during the civil rights movement in the mid twentieth century. While assistant to Robert Kennedy, he was sent to Alabama to speak with the state's governor about the safety of a group of civil rights activists known as the Freedom Riders. He was the victim of violence himself during a brutal confrontation with a group of white supremacists: As Seigenthaler was trying to protect a young female activist, a member of the Ku Klux Klan beat him with a lead pipe. During his days at the helm of *The Tennessean*, the paper was known for its bold stances on supporting civil rights, including a well-known series of articles for which one of Seigenthaler's reporters infiltrated the Klan itself. After retiring from the newspaper business, Seigenthaler founded the First Amendment Center, in part to educate the public about the importance of First Amendment values in society.

Given his long-lived devotion to civil rights and First Amendment causes, Seigenthaler was shocked when he discovered an article on Wikipedia.com that suggested he was a suspect in the assassinations of his personal friends John F. Kennedy and Robert F. Kennedy. The false biography also stated that he lived in Russia and may have been a spy. A later post on the Internet referred to him as a "vicious little turd burglar."

The offending material remained on Wikipedia for more than 120 days before it was removed, but even after that it was still accessible on the site's history pages. In a *USA Today* piece, Seigenthaler responded to the article: "And so we live in a universe of new media with phenomenal opportunities for worldwide communications and research—but populated by volunteer vandals with poison-pen intellects."[28] With regard to the history pages, he later wrote, "it's as if someone lifted the lid on a sewer."[29]

Wikipedia can be a very valuable research tool but, as Seigenthaler says, "there has to be an answer to stop the problem of misinformation."[30] It is this very problem of misinformation

John Seigenthaler *(above)*, **once an administrative assistant to Robert Kennedy, works in his office in December 2005. Earlier that year, the biographical entry on Seigenthaler was altered to include false information implicating him in the assassinations of both Robert F. Kennedy and John F. Kennedy.**

that concerns those who do wish to include bloggers into the definition of "journalist." Journalism, or at least good journalism, prides itself on accuracy—on double-checking the comments of sources, fact-checking, and various levels of editing. This checking and editing process is often extremely short-circuited in the blogosphere, where people deal in rank rumor and instantaneous journalism. There simply isn't nearly the same level of care on the Internet, and the individual can post material immediately and deal with the consequences later. For this reason, many argue that bloggers simply should not be accorded the same privileges as mainstream journalists. The idea is that the journalism profession would be devalued by including in its circle anyone who can write anything without consequences.

The U.S. Supreme Court recognizes the problem of defining who is a journalist.

There is a threshold question in this area that is recognized by the U.S. Supreme Court. That question is how to define who is a journalist for the purposes of a state shield law. The question of who is a journalist has confounded the public and the press for a long time. The U.S. Supreme Court recognized this difficulty in its 1972 decision *Branzburg v. Hayes*.[31] The case involved reporters who witnessed criminal activity and then refused to help law enforcement officials in their quest to enforce generally applicable criminal laws. The press has no special license to violate or contribute to the violation of existing laws. For this reason, a majority of the U.S. Supreme Court rejected the idea that there was a First Amendment–based privilege for reporters to withhold such information.

Part of the court's concern was that applying such a privilege would be too difficult. A primary difficulty would be determining who is entitled to the privilege. Justice Byron White wrote:

> The administration of a constitutional newsman's privilege would present practical and conceptual difficulties of a high order. Sooner or later, it would be necessary to define those categories of newsmen who qualified for the privilege, a questionable procedure in light of the traditional doctrine that liberty of the press is the right of the lonely pamphleteer who uses carbon paper or a mimeograph just as much as of the large metropolitan publisher who utilizes the latest photocomposition methods.[32]

White added:

> Freedom of the press is a "fundamental personal right" which "is not confined to newspapers and periodicals. It necessarily embraces pamphlets and leaflets. . . . The press in its historic

connotation comprehends every sort of publication which affords a vehicle of information and opinion." . . . The informative function asserted by representatives of the organized press in the present cases is also performed by lecturers, political pollsters, novelists, academic researchers, and dramatists. Almost any author may quite accurately assert that he is contributing to the flow of information to the public, that he relies on confidential sources of information, and that these sources will be silenced if he is forced to make disclosures before a grand jury.[33]

The U.S. Court of Appeals for the District of Columbia dealt with this vexing question as well in the case involving Judith Miller, a former journalist for the *New York Times*. The court examined whether there was a First Amendment–based privilege for journalists to withhold information from government officials. Judge David Sentelle wrote:

Are we then to create a privilege that protects only those reporters employed by Time Magazine, the New York Times, and other media giants, or do we extend that protection as well to the owner of a desktop printer producing a weekly newsletter to inform his neighbors, lodge brothers, co-religionists, or co-conspirators? Perhaps more to the point today, does the privilege also protect the proprietor of a web log: the stereotypical "blogger" sitting in his pajamas at his personal computer posting on the World Wide Web his best product to inform whoever happens to browse his way? If not, why not? How could one draw a distinction consistent with the court's vision of a broadly granted personal right? If so, then would it not be possible for a government official wishing to engage in the sort of unlawful leaking under investigation in the present controversy to call a trusted friend or a political ally, advise him to set up a web log (which I understand takes about three minutes) and then leak to him under a promise of confidentiality the information which the law forbids the official to disclose?[34]

Judge Sentelle is saying that one reason journalists should not have a First Amendment–based reporter privilege under the common law is because it would have to be extended to the "stereotypical blogger sitting in his pajamas." Many argue that bloggers simply don't have the built-in accountability that mainstream journalists do. Professional journalists must submit their work to a team of editors and are responsible to their employer when they write. A blogger sitting at home on his computer is beholden to no one in particular. This means that the blogger typically does not exercise the care in his craft that a responsible mainstream journalist does.

Many existing state statutes don't cover bloggers—nor should they.

Some bloggers claim that they should be protected by existing reporter shield laws. Whatever one thinks of the merits of such claims, the reality is that many (if not most) state shield laws are not written to cover bloggers. They are narrowly defined to cover those who work in traditional media. For example, Alabama's shield law provides:

> No person engaged in, connected with or employed on any newspaper, radio broadcasting station or television station, while engaged in a news-gathering capacity, shall be compelled to disclose in any legal proceeding or trial, before any court or before a grand jury of any court, before the presiding officer of any tribunal or his agent or agents or before any committee of the legislature or elsewhere the sources of any information procured or obtained by him and published in the newspaper, broadcast by any broadcasting station, or

televised by any television station on which he is engaged, connected with or employed.[35]

Arizona's law also seemingly applies only to traditional media. It confines protection to the following:

> A person engaged in newspaper, radio, television or reporto-
> rial work, or connected with or employed by a newspaper,
> radio or television station, shall not be compelled to testify
> or disclose in a legal proceeding or trial or any proceeding
> whatever, or before any jury, inquisitorial body or commis-
> sion, or before a committee of the legislature, or elsewhere,
> the source of information procured or obtained by him for
> publication in a newspaper or for broadcasting over a radio
> or television station with which he was associated or by which
> he is employed.[36]

Arkansas's law is even more restrictive. It provides:

> Before any editor, reporter, or other writer for any newspaper,
> periodical, or radio station, or publisher of any newspaper or
> periodical, or manager or owner of any radio station shall
> be required to disclose to any grand jury or to any other
> authority the source of information used as the basis for any
> article he may have written, published, or broadcast, it must
> be shown that the article was written, published, or broad-
> cast in bad faith, with malice, and not in the interest of the
> public welfare.[37]

These laws apply to the established media that has an infra-
structure in place to ensure a degree of accuracy and responsibility. True, mainstream media reporters make mistakes and
sometimes commit libel, but there is at least a system in place
to prevent such conduct. Most bloggers do not have this type

of institutional constraint. In fact, many bloggers have no con-straints at all.

Some federal legislators recognize that extending the First Amendment-based reporter privilege protection to bloggers could cause problems. Senator John Cornyn (R.-Tex.), one of the main supporters of a federal shield law, has some reservations about extending such protection to bloggers. Senator Patrick Leahy (D.-Ver.) recognized the problem of extending any would-be protections to bloggers in a Senate judiciary committee hear-ing in October 2005:

> While a small number of cases have garnered significant national attention, the question of whether or not to enact

Quotable: Senator John Cornyn

We also need to have a serious discussion of what constitutes the term "reporter." Media consumers no longer rely exclusively on traditional media outlets to obtain information. Today's technology allows for anyone to report information to a vast audience virtually instantaneously, thus creating a new generation of "cyber reporters" or those we know today as bloggers.

At our last hearing, one of our witnesses described bloggers as the modern day equivalent of the revolutionary pamphleteer who passed out news bulletins on the street corner. However, the relative anonymity afforded to bloggers, coupled with a certain lack of accountability, as they are not your traditional brick-and-mortar reporters who answer to an editor or publisher, also has the risk of creating a certain irresponsibility when it comes to accurately reporting information.

Therefore as we consider what protections to afford, it is also important to consider whether bloggers, or reporters for entities such as *al Jazeera*, or others whose associations perhaps are questionable or even cause for concern, ought to be covered under this type of law.

Source: John Cornyn, speaking to the Senate Judiciary Committee, on Oct. 19, 2005. http://judiciary.senate.gov/member_statement.cfm?id=1637&wit_id=3740.

some form of privilege for journalists has vexed us since *Branzburg v. Hayes* was decided by the Supreme Court in 1972. Since that time, 31 states and the District of Columbia have enacted statutes granting some form of privilege to journalists. Efforts have been made from time to time to codify a reporter's privilege in federal law, but these attempts failed, in part because supporters of the concept found it difficult to agree on how to define the scope of what it means to be a "journalist." With bloggers now participating fully in the 24-hour news cycle, we might face similar challenges in defining terms today.[38]

The problem for mainstream reporters is that bloggers are making it more difficult for them to obtain a federal shield law.

Even some diehard First Amendment supporters question whether bloggers should be covered by reporter shield laws. Such people worry whether expanding the coverage will dilute the protections for the established press. "It is a very tough issue whether you include bloggers in a federal shield law," says Robert

Media Critic David Shaw

Bloggers require no journalistic experience. All they need is computer access and the desire to blog. There are other, even important differences between bloggers and mainstream journalists, perhaps the most significant being that bloggers pride themselves on being part of an unmediated medium, giving their readers unfiltered information. And therein lies the problem.

When I or virtually any other mainstream journalist writes something, it goes through several filters before the reader sees it. At least four experienced *Times* editors will have examined this column, for example. They will have checked it for accuracy, fairness, grammar, taste and libel, among other things.

Source: David Shaw, "Media Matters; Do Bloggers Deserve Basic Journalistic Protection?" *Los Angeles Times*. (March 27, 2005): p. E14.

O'Neil, founder of the Thomas Jefferson Center for the Protection of Free Expression. "It is a tough issue because often you don't know where to draw lines between bloggers and everyone else. If bloggers are protected, does that dilute the value of protection for mainstream journalists? There is a commendable desire to make the shield law meaningful by confining its scope to those who need it most. I share the ambivalence that some express on this difficult question."[39]

L.A. Times media critic David Shaw argues that many bloggers—though not all, and perhaps not most—do not appear to worry about accuracy. "They just want to get their opinions—and their 'scoops'—out there as fast as they pop into their brains," Shaw said. "One of the great advantages of the Internet, many Web lovers have told me, is that it's easy to correct an error there. You can do it instantly, as soon as the error is called to your attention instead of having to wait until the next day's paper."[40] But if a writer places information online quickly without worrying about accuracy, it will lead to falsehoods, defamatory statements, and other civil wrongs. An essential ethical principle of journalism is to strive for accuracy. Too many in the blogosphere ignore this fundamental principle. Shaw explains: ". . . the knowledge that you can correct errors quickly, combined with the absence of editors or filters, encourages laziness, carelessness, and inaccuracy, and I don't think the reporter's privilege to maintain confidential sources should be granted to such practitioners of what is at best pseudo-journalism."[41]

Summary

Many bloggers are not engaged in journalism at all. They provide their personal opinions but do not gather news in the traditional sense. Most blogs are nothing more than personal rants and places to gossip. A 2004 poll from MIT showed that more than 80 percent of them were nothing more than "personal musings."[42] Before any blogger receives the protections of the traditional press, that blogger should be required to show that he or she adheres to certain standards of conduct and engages in some type of reportorial practice.

Unfortunately, bloggers are making it much more difficult for even deserving mainstream journalists to obtain a federal shield law. The reason is that most bloggers do not behave as responsibly as the mainstream press.

Employees Should Have the Right to Blog Without Fear of Reprisal From Employers

A disgruntled employee dislikes his bosses, some of his co-workers, and many of the policies at his workplace. Instead of venting over the telephone to his family and friends, he posts his thoughts online, on his own blog. Unfortunately, he tells a co-worker about his blog and then word spreads like wildfire through his workplace. His superiors learn of the blog, read it, and find it offensive. They fire the employee for the disparaging comments he made on the blog. They claim that the employee breached a fundamental duty of loyalty and violated terms of his employment agreement.

This is a reality for many employees who at some point choose to air their grievances online. The new medium of the Internet makes one person's comments much more accessible, potentially viewable worldwide. Employers do not want to see dirty laundry aired publicly. Many employees have been fired for their blogging activities even if the blogging is done entirely off duty, using no company facilities or computers. Employee bloggers must beware if they blog about something that their company considers offensive, inappropriate, disloyal, or disturbing.

Consider the case of Rachel Mosteller who worked for the newspaper the *Herald Sun* in Durham, North Carolina. Mosteller wrote on her blog under the name "Sarcastic Journalist." A sample of her posting:

> I really hate my place of employment. Seriously. Okay, first off. They have these stupid little awards that are supposed to boost company morale. So you go and do something "spectacular" (most likely, you're doing your JOB) and then someone says, "Why golly, that was spectacular." then they sign your name on some paper, they bring you chocolate and some balloons.
>
> Okay two people in the newsroom just got it. FOR DOING THEIR JOB.[43]

She was fired only one day after this appeared on her blog.

Mosteller is not alone. Other employees have faced similar reactions. In fact, employers have terminated enough employees for their blogging activities that it has added another word to the English language: "doocing." Blogger Heather B. Armstrong coined the term after she was fired from her job for writing on her blog Dooce.com.[44]

Ellen Simonetti was a competent flight attendant for Delta Airlines; however, Delta reacted negatively after viewing pictures of Simonetti on her Web site "Queen of Sky." The photos included Simonetti posing in her uniform, and Delta felt the photos were inappropriate and terminated her. She continues writing on her Web site and even wrote a book entitled *Diary of a Dysfunctional Flight Attendant: Queen of Sky Blog.* She responded to her termination by starting a "Blogger Rights Movement" on her Web site. She explained in an interview:

> That was my brainchild in January of 2005, a few months after I was fired. The goal was to try to humiliate companies who had fired bloggers by posting their names on a list on the

From the Colorado State Legislature, on Employee Blogging

24-34-402.5. Unlawful prohibition of legal activities as a condition of employment:

(1) It shall be a discriminatory or unfair employment practice for an employer to terminate the employment of any employee due to that employee's engaging in any lawful activity off the premises of the employer during nonworking hours unless such a restriction:

    (a) Relates to a bona fide occupational requirement or is reasonably and rationally related to the employment activities and responsibilities of a particular employee or a particular group of employees, rather than to all employees of the employer; or

    (b) Is necessary to avoid a conflict of interest with any responsibilities to the employer or the appearance of such a conflict of interest.

(2) (a) Notwithstanding any other provisions of this article, the sole remedy for any person claiming to be aggrieved by a discriminatory or unfair employment practice as defined in this section shall be as follows: He may bring a civil suit for damages in any district court of competent jurisdiction and may sue for all wages and benefits which would have been due him up to and including the date of the judgment had the discriminatory or unfair employment practice not occurred; except that nothing in this section shall be construed to relieve such person from the obligation to mitigate his damages.

    (b) The court shall award the prevailing party in such action court costs and a reasonable attorney fee.

Source: C.R.S. 24-34-402.5 (2006).

Internet. I also had a declaration there that stated something like "no blogger should be fired." I still believe that no blogger should be fired without first being given a warning, although there are some situations where it might be called for [i.e., specific physical threats against a coworker or racial slurs where the company's name is involved].[45]

Peter Whitney was another casualty of blogging. Whitney worked for Wells Fargo in their mailroom and lost his job after his bosses learned that he criticized fellow employees on his blog. "Right now it's too gray," Whitney told *USA Today*. "There needs to be clearer guidelines. Some people go to a bar and complain about workers. I decided to do it online. Some people say I deserve what happened, but it was really harsh. It was unfair."[46]

The First Amendment limits the ability of public employers to punish off-duty employee speech.

Employees who work for the federal, state, or local government—public employees—retain some level of First Amendment protection. Or, stated another way, public employers must operate within the constraints of the Bill of Rights, including the First Amendment.

The First Amendment—the first 45 words of the Bill of Rights—provides that government officials will not "abridge the freedom of speech." Public employees give up some of their constitutional rights when they enter the workplace. A public employee does not have a constitutional right to walk around her office and say, "My boss is a complete idiot"; however, a public employee does not lose all his rights as a citizen simply because he has accepted public employment. The U.S. Supreme Court has ruled that public employees have a right to speak out on important matters of public concern.

The old view was that public employees forfeited all constitutional rights when they accepted public employment. Justice Oliver Wendell Holmes expressed this view in the late nineteenth century, when he was a justice on the Massachusetts Supreme Judicial Court (before he became a justice on the U.S. Supreme Court). The case in question, *McAuliffe v. Town of Bedford*, involved a police officer who was fired for his political expression. Holmes rejected the police officer's First Amendment claim, explaining, "The petitioner (police officer) may have a constitutional right to talk politics, but he has no constitutional right to be a policeman."[47]

The U.S. Supreme Court changed this jurisprudence, ruling that public employees do not lose all of their First Amendment rights when they accept public employment. In *Pickering v. Board of Education* (1968), the court ruled that junior high school teacher Marvin Pickering's First Amendment rights were violated when his school district terminated him for writing a letter to the editor to the local newspaper that was critical of the school district's allocation of money vis-à-vis academics and athletics. In a 2001 interview, Pickering recalled:

> Members of the board were not being straight about how they were spending some of this money for these new schools. They were spending too much money on athletics. Instead of spending $3.2 million at one school and $2.3 million at the other school, they spent more than $4 million on one of the schools. As a result the classrooms at Lockport East were constructed with three walls. This was a nightmare for teachers as the rooms opened into each other.[48]

Other statements in his 1964 letter included:

- "That's the kind of totalitarianism teachers live in at the high school, and your children go to school in."

- "But $20,000 in receipts doesn't pay for the $200,000 a year they have been spending on varsity sports while neglecting the wants of teachers."

- "To sod football fields on borrowed money and then not be able to pay teachers' salaries is getting the cart before the horse."

- "As I see it, the bond issue is a fight between the Board of Education that is trying to push tax-supported athletics down our throats with education, and a public that has mixed emotions about both of these items because they feel they are already paying enough taxes, and simply don't know whom to trust with any more tax money."[49]

Pickering challenged his dismissal in court and eventually prevailed four years later in the U.S. Supreme Court. Justice Thurgood Marshall wrote in the Supreme Court decision: "The problem in any case is to arrive at a balance between the interests of the teacher, as a citizen, in commenting upon matters of public concern and the interest of the State, as an employer, in promoting the efficiency of the public services it performs through its employees."[50]

The court determined that Marvin Pickering's right to free speech outweighed the school district's interests in avoiding controversy. Justice Marshall also pointed out that teachers like Pickering are in the best position to speak about matters of public importance involving education. "Teachers are, as a class, the members of a community most likely to have informed and definite opinions as to how funds allotted to the operation of the schools should be spent," Marshall said.[51]

Since the *Pickering* decision, public employees have been accorded some level of First Amendment rights. If public employees speak out on matters of public concern, they have free-speech protection as long as their rights are not outweighed by the employers' interest in an efficient, disruption-free workplace. The court has made clear that if a public employee speaks more as a citizen than as an employee, the employer has limited control over the employee's speech activities. In *Garcetti v. Ceballos* (2006), however, the Court provided that public employees have no First Amendment protection for speech that is part of their official job duties.

A public employee blogging about an important public issue may well be protected by the First Amendment, particularly if the blogging is done off duty on the employee's own time. Public employees speak more as citizens than employees when they blog on their own time. Employers who try to discipline employees for legal, off-duty expression must meet a very high threshold and show that somehow the employee's expression impairs working relationships. As long as the speech constitutes a matter of public importance and is not

From the Connecticut State Legislature: Liability of Employer for Discipline or Discharge of Employee on Account of Employee's Exercise of Certain Constitutional Rights

Any employer, including the state and any instrumentality or political subdivision thereof, who subjects any employee to discipline or discharge on account of the exercise by such employee of rights guaranteed by the *First Amendment to the United States Constitution* or section 3, 4 or 14 of article first of the Constitution of the state, provided such activity does not substantially or materially interfere with the employee's bona fide job performance or the working relationship between the employee and the employer, shall be liable to such employee for damages caused by such discipline or discharge, including punitive damages, and for reasonable attorney's fees as part of the costs of any such action for damages. If the court determines that such action for damages was brought without substantial justification, the court may award costs and reasonable attorney's fees to the employer.

Source: Conn. Gen. Stat. § 31-51q.

inherently disruptive, the public employee has a right to free speech—including a right to blog—and should not lose his or her job.

Even private employees should not lose all rights when blogging.

Unfortunately, First Amendment protections for public employees does not cover many individuals in the nation's workforce. Most employees work in the private sector, which mean that they do not work for the government. The First Amendment provides no protection of free speech for private employees. Legal commentator Henry Hoang Pham warns,

> Bloggers should beware—employers can, and have, discharged employees at-will for blogging. . . . Furthermore, nothing prevents an employer from not hiring a potential employee because of his blog. Thus, bloggers should exercise the same, if not greater, decorum and restraint online as they would on the telephone or through e-mail, because their professional careers may be at stake.[52]

Professor Robert Sprague reaches a similar conclusion. "Based on current employment law," Sprague wrote, "employees who blog are best advised to heed the caveat: bloggers beware."[53]

Most private employees are subject to the employment-at-will doctrine. This doctrine means that either the employer or employee can terminate the employment relationship whenever desired. The doctrine favors employers because it means that employers can fire employees for any reason—a good reason, a bad one, or no reason at all. The Tennessee Supreme Court explained the rationale of the doctrine in 1884 when it wrote: "Men must be left, without interference to buy and sell where they please, and to discharge or retain employees at-will for good cause or for no cause, or even for bad cause without thereby being guilty of an unlawful act per se."[54]

The doctrine presumes that employers and employees have equal bargaining power. This is a false assumption. In the vast majority of cases, employers wield much more power, as many employees live paycheck to paycheck and cannot afford to quit their jobs whenever they want. These employees also cannot challenge employer policies without suffering financial hardships.

There are growing exceptions to the employment-at-will doctrine.

Some states have recognized numerous exceptions to the employment-at-will doctrine. These include the covenant of good faith and fair dealing, contractual exceptions to employment at will and various public policy exceptions. The covenant of good faith and fair dealing prohibits employers from terminating employees for weak reasons; it generally requires employers to show just cause before terminating an employee.[55] Furthermore, some employees may be covered by an employment contract or by implied contractual promises of continued employment. These exceptions are entirely state-specific. Some states have broader exceptions to the at-will doctrine, while other states are called "at-will" states because they recognize few or no exceptions.

Some employees may be protected for their blogging if the content of their blogging constitutes "whistle blowing"—calling out unlawful employer conduct. For example, if a private prison employee blogs on her Web site about the horrors of inmate brutality or guard–inmate sexual relations, this employee is blowing the whistle on corruption.[56] Such speech should be protected.

The National Labor Relations Act may protect employees who blog about labor conditions in their workforce. Such blogging may fit within the definition of "concerted activity." Professor Katherine M. Scott explains that:

> . . . various laws limit an employer's control over what employees write, especially outside of working hours. One such

law is the National Labor Relations Act ("NLRA"), which protects certain activities by non-supervisory private sector employees. Specifically, section 7 of the NLRA protects "the right . . . to form, join, or assist labor organizations . . . and to engage in other concerted activities for the purpose of collective bargaining or other mutual aid or protection." Employers may not "interfere with, restrain, or coerce employees in the exercise of" their section 7 rights. These provisions likely extend to employee blogs under certain circumstances.[57]

Public policy exceptions generally include specific statutes or laws that spell out such an exception. For example, many states have laws that prohibit employers from terminating employees for serving on jury duty or for reporting illegal activities in the workplace. Some states have broader public policy exceptions, which may recognize a generalized right to privacy or a right to freedom from being fired for legal, off-duty conduct or expression. One such state is Connecticut, whose state law

From the North Dakota State Legislature: Employer's Discriminatory Practices

It is a discriminatory practice for an employer to fail or refuse to hire a person; to discharge an employee; or to accord adverse or unequal treatment to a person or employee with respect to application, hiring, training, apprenticeship, tenure, promotion, upgrading, compensation, layoff, or a term, privilege, or condition of employment, because of race, color, religion, sex, national origin, age, physical or mental disability, status with respect to marriage or public assistance, or participation in lawful activity off the employer's premises during nonworking hours which is not in direct conflict with the essential business-related interests of the employer.

Source: N.D. Cent. Code, § 14-02.4-03 (2007).

prohibits employers in the state from terminating employees for speech that would be protected under the First Amendment or the state constitution. This is a progressive stance on the subject, and more states should follow suit.

Summary

The above-referenced state laws provide a baseline of protection for employees who blog while off duty. More states should consider adopting similar laws. Many states have laws that prohibit employers from terminating employees because they smoke off duty. There should not be less protection for employees who speak out in their blogs.

It is hoped that this area of the law will catch up to reality and provide the necessary protection for employees. Many employee-bloggers are in the best position to inform the public about pressing societal issues. They know the issues because their employment puts them in the center of the areas about which they write. There is a strong First Amendment–based interest in allowing these people to blog without fear of reprisal. There are obvious exceptions for character assassination, but there should be a baseline level of protection for employee-bloggers.

Employers Should Have Wide Latitude to Discipline Bloggers for Comments Detrimental to the Workplace

A disgruntled employee believes that he was unfairly passed over for a promotion. The employee decides to vent online, criticizing his employer on his personal blog. The online diary goes beyond simple criticism and talks about the private lives of co-workers and supervisors. The blog also contains false statements of fact that harm the reputations of others. In other words, the blog contains libelous material. Libel is a *tort*—a civil cause of action in which the normal remedy is monetary damages. In the law, an employer is often legally responsible for the tortious actions committed by his or her employees.

But it gets worse in this particular scenario: The employee also sends material to his employer's competitors, revealing trade secrets and key customer lists. The blogger also sends spam messages to many of the corporation's customers, lowering the corporation's reputation. The spam messages contain links to the employee's blog, which again, contains false statements of fact. The employer disciplines the employee, but the employee continues to vent online. The employer then terminates the employee—for good reason. Employees may think that whatever they do on their own time makes them immune from employer discipline. In the vast majority of workplaces in the United States, however, that assumption would be incorrect.

Employers have the right to terminate employees for conduct detrimental to the company. The actions of the hypothetical employee described above would likely be just cause for termination.

Employers have many legitimate concerns about employee blogging.

Employers have many legitimate concerns with the content of employee blogs. First and foremost, an employee's blogging could create liability for the company. Legal commentator Paul S. Gutman explains:

> The first such concern is the employer's fear of and potential liability for criminal activity. An employer is right to worry about an employee guilty of online libel through or on his or her blog, just as he or she may be concerned about a letter to the editor or any other defamatory statement. Since many blogs consider political topics and public figures, libelous statements may easily be made. Likewise, a blogger providing links to illegal works or pornographic material might jeopardize his employer or the employer's relationship with others.[58]

Legal commentators Lichtenstein and Darrow write, "employers have a legitimate interest in discouraging employee behavior (including blogs and other electronic communications) that may result in substantial liability for the employer."[59] Generally speaking, an employer is liable for torts perpetrated by its employees. If an employee's blog included defamatory falsehoods about a competitor, the competitor may well sue not only the offending blogger but also the blogger's employer—particularly if the employee used an office computer or was acting as an employee in some capacity when he made the false statements.

Gutman notes numerous other concerns that an employer may have, including: "diversion of corporate resources," "violation of contractual covenants" between employers and employees, and concerns about the reputation of the company.[60] He adds that "employers ... are likely to be concerned about a blog's potential impact on their company's image with people they work for and with, as well as with the people that work for them."[61]

Employer concern with employee blogs extends beyond the conduct of the actual employee. The concern extends to any third person who contributes to the employee's blog. Lichtenstein and Darrow explain:

> Another potential major area of concern for the employer is where third parties post comments on the employee's blog that contain defamatory, obscene or pornographic material, violate the employer's legal rights or interests, or constitute an invasion of the employer's privacy. The major issue here is one of assigning liability for content beyond the author of the blog.[62]

Employers also have a broad right to discipline employee-bloggers who violate the fundamental duty of loyalty. Unfortunately, many of the most vehement anti-employer bloggers hide behind the shield of anonymity, as the Internet affords persons the ability to communicate anonymously. Legal commentator Konrad Lee writes that employers should have the broadest authority to pursue claims and discipline against those employees who violate the duty of loyalty on their blogs. He writes:

> The rise of Internet blogs has created a new and powerful information tool on the internet. The authors of anti-employer

blogs often hide behind anonymity to disclose confidential information about the employer or engage in disloyal anti-employer blogging. The employer has a right to pursue breach of the duty of loyalty claims against such persons and the anonymity of the internet should not protect bloggers because tortious anti-employer speech is not protected by law.[63]

The First Amendment does not protect employees when their blogging impairs working relationships.

Many individuals operate under the mistaken assumption that they have a right to free speech that includes blogging without repercussions. People naturally assume that they have some sort of basic legal right to do what they want, as long as they are off duty. This assumption is fundamentally wrong for several reasons.

First, private employees—those employees who do not work for the federal, state, or local government—have no federal constitutional protections. The Bill of Rights of the U.S. Constitution protects people from invasion of their constitutional rights by the government only. This is the state action doctrine, meaning that there must be a governmental trigger to state a valid constitutional claim. This means that private employees have no First Amendment rights vis-à-vis their employer.

In fact, many private employees are no more than at-will employees. This means that they can be fired at will by their employer and, conversely, they can also quit at will. The theory behind the at-will employment doctrine is that either party—the employer or the employee—can terminate the working relationship at will. There are exceptions to this doctrine, though. An employer cannot fire an employee because of the employee's race or sex. In some states, employers cannot fire employees because of their sexual orientation. In most states, an employer cannot fire an employee over a workers' compensation claim or because the employee reported illegal activity, had their wages garnished, or served on a jury.

There is no blogging exception to the employment-at-will doctrine. In other words, private employees can be terminated for blogging. Labor attorney Gregg M. Lemley told the *Washington Post*, "In most states, if an employer doesn't like what you're talking about, they can simply terminate you."[64]

Consider the analogous case of *Marsh v. Delta Air Lines, Inc.*[65] Michael Marsh had been employed by Delta Air Lines as a baggage handler for 26 years. He was terminated after he wrote a letter to the editor of the *Denver Post* that criticized Delta's decision to hire hourly contract labor to replace full-time employees who had been laid off. Marsh asserted a wrongful termination claim, but the federal court ruled in favor of Delta Air Lines. The federal court ruled that Marsh violated an implied duty of loyalty to his employer by criticizing the employer so harshly. Such conduct justified his termination, as he had a "special job responsibility of promoting a positive image for Delta."[66]

Private employee-bloggers can be terminated just as easily as Marsh was for his letter to the newspaper. Blogs are as public as a newspaper, if not more so. Material on a blog has the potential to be viewed by a much wider audience than a newspaper of general circulation.

Even public employers have broad discretion to terminate employee bloggers.

Unlike their counterparts in the private sector, public employees do possess at least some First Amendment rights when they accept public employment. Public employers must act in accordance with the Bill of Rights, including the First Amendment; however, the U.S. Supreme Court has made clear that public employers have wide latitude to discipline employees who engage in expression that creates disruption, disharmony, or upsets working relationships. Even the foundational decision that established public employees' First Amendment rights to free speech—*Pickering v. Board of Education*—emphasized that protected speech must not impair close working relationships. Although the court in *Pickering* ruled that teacher Marvin Pickering had a First Amendment right as a citizen-employee to write a letter to the editor, the court emphasized that Pickering did not make statements that would impair his day-to-day working relationships. The court explained:

> The statements are in no way directed towards any person with whom appellant would normally be in contact in the course of his daily work as a teacher. Thus no question of maintaining either discipline by immediate superiors or harmony among coworkers is presented here. Appellant's employment relationships with the Board and, to a somewhat lesser extent, with the superintendent are not the kind of close working relationships for which it can persuasively be claimed that personal loyalty and confidence are necessary to their proper functioning.[67]

In order to state a valid First Amendment claim, a public employee first must establish that he or she was speaking more as a citizen than as an employee. Then, the employee must establish that his or her speech touched on a matter of public concern or public importance. Many public employee speech claims are dismissed because the employee's speech was merely a personal grievance, as opposed to a statement about a broader public issue. One federal appeals court explained: "When a public employee's speech is purely job-related, that speech will not be deemed a matter of public concern. Unless the employee is speaking as a concerned citizen, and not just as an employee, the speech does not fall under the protection of the First Amendment."[68] Thus, if a public employee-blogger simply gripes about his job, this speech receives no First Amendment protection because it doesn't touch on a matter of public concern. It is simply a personal grievance.

Even if a public employee passes the threshold public concern requirement, the employee must then show that his or her free-speech interests outweigh the employer's interests in an efficient, disruption-free workplace. This balancing prong requires deference to employers, as the courts are not supposed to serve as super-personnel departments. "Sometimes courts will defer to employers' judgments about the potential disruptiveness of employee speech."[69] The U.S. Supreme Court made this clear in *Connick v. Myers*: "When close working relationships are essential to fulfilling public responsibilities, a wide degree of deference to the employer's judgment is appropriate. Furthermore, we do not see the necessity for an employer to allow events to unfold to the extent that the disruption of the office and the destruction of working relationships is manifest before taking action."[70]

The Supreme Judicial Court of Massachusetts ruled in *Pereira v. Commission of Social Services* that a city employee

---

FROM THE BENCH

U.S. Supreme Court Justice Byron White

When a public employee speaks not as a citizen upon matters of public concern, but instead as an employee upon matters only of personal interest, absent the most unusual circumstances, a federal court is not the appropriate forum in which to review the wisdom of a personnel decision taken by a public agency allegedly in reaction to the employee's behavior. Cf. *Bishop v. Wood, supra,* at 349–350. Our responsibility is to ensure that citizens are not deprived of fundamental rights by virtue of working for the government; this does not require a grant of immunity for employee grievances not afforded by the First Amendment to those who do not work for the State.... To presume that all matters which transpire within a government office are of public concern would mean that virtually every remark—and certainly every criticism directed at a public official—would plant the seed of a constitutional case. While, as a matter of good judgment, public officials should be receptive to constructive criticism offered by their employees, the First Amendment does not require a public office to be run as a roundtable for employee complaints over internal office affairs.

Source: *Connick v. Myers,* 461 U.S. 138 (1983).

Supreme Court associate justice Byron White is shown in this photograph from 1993. White served on the Court from 1962 until his retirement in 1993.

could be fired for telling a racial joke at a party while off duty.[71] "Pereira's 'racist' comment (as she herself characterizes it) undermined those goals [of maintaining a disruption-free workplace]," the court wrote. "The commissioner was understandably

concerned about the appearance of racial bias in the department's investigators. At the very least Pereira exhibited outstandingly poor judgment, and poor judgment is inconsistent with difficulties that investigators face every day."[72] The court noted the fact that the employee was in an important position of authority, such that her remarks reflected negatively upon the entire department.

Pereira demonstrates that the courts recognize even a public employer's right to sanction an employee for speech under certain circumstances; it is easily applicable to employee blogging. Even advocates of free speech recognize that employee blogging that leads to disruptions in the workplace are problematic and likely open the employee up to sanction. Kurt Opsahl explains:

> If you work for any level of government, your employer's right to fire you is also limited by the First Amendment's protection of your right to free speech. However, your free-speech rights as an employee are more limited than they are as a member of the general public. If you were to challenge your termination on First Amendment grounds, courts would balance your employer's legitimate interest in delivering efficient government services against your interest as a citizen in commenting on a matter of public concern. So if you blog about something important to the public, you have greater protection. But if your blog's content could disrupt the workplace, your protection diminishes.[73]

Summary

Citizens generally can blog free from governmental interference; however, they don't have the same level of rights when they accept employment, since employers have legitimate interests to protect as well. An employee can be fired for calling one of his bosses a moron or an idiot. An employee can also be fired if the speech occurs online at a blog—the employer retains the same interests in ensuring that the workplace runs smoothly and efficiently.

Private employees have little recourse when their employer reasonably punishes them for comments on a blog that are detrimental to the company, its products, or its image. The employment-at-will doctrine ensures a wide degree of deference to employers in business judgments.

Even public employees must be careful when they blog about their job, their co-workers, or their superiors. Close working relationships can be impaired by negative comments posted online. Public employers have broad latitude to discipline employees whose blogging causes negative repercussions at work.

Many agree with journalist Dan Cordtz's assertion that employee blogging and the negativity surrounding some of them are "becoming a growing legal and personnel headache for employers across the nation."[74]

School Officials Don't Have Authority to Regulate Students' Off-Campus Blogging

"There is no legal justification for censoring a student's expression in the privacy of his home."

—Ken Paulson[75]

"Suppression of speech may reduce security as well as liberty."

—Judge Andrew Kleinfeld[76]

In Taft High School in Chicago, Illinois, school officials suspended three students for what school officials deemed to be threatening and offensive comments about school officials. One teacher apparently cried after reading the material on the students' blog. Many students, however, believed that the school overreacted by punishing the students with 10-day suspensions. Many students also believed that the school didn't have the power in the first place to punish students for expression that was created entirely off campus.

According to the *Chicago Sun-Times*, the issue has divided the school community. "A blog is like your journal," one student explained. "You should be able to say whatever you want in it and not worry about getting in trouble, especially because it's done on your own time and not in school."[77] Likewise, another student explained: "It's none of their business. Why are they monitoring online student journals in the first place? You would think teachers and staff have better things to do, like making this school a better place. . . . I think they had no right to read it, much less suspend those students."[78]

Colorado ACLU Press Release

"I am pleased that Littleton school officials were willing to resolve this dispute without a lawsuit," said Hugh Gottschalk, an ACLU cooperating attorney whose firm worked over the 3-day weekend on Mr. Lopez's case. "A student's right of expression is protected by the First Amendment. School authorities have some ability to regulate students' expressive activities on school grounds and at school-related functions. But school authorities do not have the right to impose discipline for statements that students make off campus, especially when, as in this case, those statements do not cause any material disruption of the educational process."

"Mr. Lopez used his home computer to post his commentary on the web site MySpace.com on February 7," explained Mark Silverstein, ACLU Legal Director. The message contained satirical commentary about the poor physical condition of Littleton High School, the behavior and demographics of students and staff, the perceived racial biases of teachers and administrators, and the poor quality of the resources available to students.

Source: ACLU of Colorado press release. "After ACLU Intervention, High School Student Suspended for Off-campus Internet Posting Is Back in School." http://www.aclu-co.org/news/pressrelease/release_myspace.htm.

Unfortunately, school officials *are* monitoring and punishing students for the content of their blogs. If a student writes something critical of school officials, that student could very well face punishment. That is what happened to Colorado high school student Bryan Lopez after he wrote a satirical piece about his school online. Lopez mocked the poor physical conditions of the school, the behavior of students, the lack of school resources, and other issues he deemed important. School officials suspended him for this even though they failed to show any evidence that his speech caused any type of disruption at school. The American Civil Liberties Union assisted Lopez, threatening the school with a lawsuit. The school ended up backing down and allowed Lopez to return to school.[79]

School officials do not have jurisdiction over off-campus student expression.

Many students have turned to the Internet to express a variety of viewpoints, including criticism of school officials. The First Amendment protects critical speech posted on the Internet. No less an authority than the U.S. Supreme Court in *Reno v. ACLU* (1997) wrote that speech on the Internet is entitled to the highest level of protection, on a par with the print medium.[80] The late First Amendment attorney Bruce Ennis hailed the decision as granting the Internet its "legal birth certificate."[81]

Unfortunately, the actions of some school officials have not respected students' First Amendment–protected expression. Instead, they have led to a clamping down on student expression. Justin Layshock was a Pennsylvania high school student suspended from school for lampooning his principal on a MySpace page he created while at his grandmother's house. Justin and his parents sued the school, alleging a violation of his First Amendment rights because he was punished for content that he created at home. Layshock and his parents contended that he should not be punished for off-campus conduct or expression.

The family sued "because of the type of punishment that Justin received," explained Justin's mother, Cheryl. After the suspension, "They placed him in alternative school and gave him no access to the classroom. We were going to let them get away with the 10-day suspension, even though we disagreed with that, as well. We believed this was a matter of parental discipline, and we punished Justin ourselves." When asked whether school officials should punish students for off-campus behavior, she responded: "No, we punished Justin for what he did. Schools should punish students for what they do at school."[82]

This threshold question of on-campus versus off-campus expression is vitally important: There is an argument that if the expression takes place off-campus, school officials simply do not have jurisdiction over a student's speech. Many of the student online cases should be matters of parental discipline, not school discipline.

A case involving the physical world, as opposed to the online world, is instructive. In *Klein v. Smith* (1986), a federal district court in Maine examined whether school officials were justified in suspending a public school student for 10 days for making a vulgar gesture (extending the middle finger) at a teacher at a local restaurant.[83] The school determined that it had the authority to discipline the student for off-campus conduct and charged him with violating a rule prohibiting "vulgar or extremely inappropriate language or conduct directed to a staff member." The student disagreed, contending that school officials overstepped their authority. A federal district court sided with the student, noting that the conduct occurred off campus, "far removed from any school premises or facilities." The court reasoned that school officials overreached in disciplining "the digital posturing of this splenetic, bad-mannered little boy" and concluded that any connection between the student's disrespectful actions to the orderly operation of the school was "too attenuated." This case stands for the principle that school officials do not have jurisdiction over student expression that takes place away from school grounds. *Klein v. Smith* could provide legal authority for the principle that school officials do not have the power to censor student online expression created off campus.

Ann Beeson, a leading civil liberties lawyer, says that schools punishing students for off-campus online expression is one of the major "disturbing trends" in the school law arena. "In many cases, especially since the Littleton [Columbine High School] tragedy, school officials are punishing students for their online speech," she says. "If a student publishes material on his home computer, that is the parents' jurisdiction, not the school's. It is an intrusion on the parent-child relationship."[84]

Similarly, Raymond Vasvari, legal director for the American Civil Liberties Union of Ohio, said: "There is no U.S. Supreme Court precedent for the principle that students enjoy diminished First Amendment rights when they are off-campus simply by virtue of being young. When students are engaging in expression off campus, they are wearing the hat of a young citizen, not of a student."[85]

Public school students do retain First Amendment rights at school.

Although there is no U.S. Supreme Court precedent for limiting off-campus student speech, there is precedent for the fundamental principle that public school students do not lose their First Amendment rights when they are students. In *Tinker v. Des Moines Independent Community School District*, the U.S. Supreme Court ruled that public school officials in Des Moines, Iowa, violated the First Amendment rights of several students when they suspended them for wearing black armbands to school to protest U.S. involvement in the Vietnam War.[86] The court wrote that students do not "shed their constitutional rights to freedom of speech and expression at the schoolhouse gate."[87]

The court established the so-called *Tinker* standard. This standard provides that school officials can censor student expression only if they can reasonably forecast that the expression will create a real interference, will cause a substantial disruption of the educational environment, or will invade the rights of others. The high court reasoned that school officials could not silence student expression simply because of "undifferentiated fear or apprehension."[88]

The fundamental lesson from *Tinker* is that school officials should not censor student blogging simply out of such "undifferentiated fear."

FROM THE BENCH

The U.S. Supreme Court in *Tinker v. Des Moines Indep. Comm. School District*, 393 U.S. 503 (1969)

In our system, undifferentiated fear or apprehension of disturbance is not enough to overcome the right to freedom of expression. Any departure from absolute regimentation may cause trouble. Any variation from the majority's opinion may inspire fear. Any word spoken, in class, in the lunchroom, or on the campus, that deviates from the views of another person may start an argument or cause a disturbance. But our Constitution says we must take this risk . . . and our history says that it is this sort of hazardous freedom—this kind of openness—that is the basis of our national strength and of the independence and vigor of Americans who grow up and live in this relatively permissive, often disputatious, society. . . .

In our system, state-operated schools may not be enclaves of totalitarianism.

School officials do not possess absolute authority over their students. Students in school as well as out of school are "persons" under our Constitution. They are possessed of fundamental rights which the State must respect, just as they themselves must respect their obligations to the State. In our system, students may not be regarded as closed-circuit recipients of only that which the State chooses to communicate. They may not be confined to the expression of those sentiments that are officially approved. In the absence of a specific showing of constitutionally valid reasons to regulate their speech, students are entitled to freedom of expression of their views.

Some lower courts have ruled that school officials have gone too far in punishing students for online expression.

Numerous lower courts have recognized that school officials violate the First Amendment when they punish public school students for their online expression. Consider the case of *Beussink v. Woodland R-IV School District.*[89] Brandon Beussink, then a junior at Woodland High School in Missouri, created his own homepage on his own computer at his own home. The homepage was critical of the school administration and included vulgar language in his opinions of teachers and the principal. A student showed Beussink's page to a teacher at school. The teacher, upset by the content of the Web site, informed the principal. The principal initially suspended Beussink for five days because he was offended by the content on the site, and he later extended the suspension to twice that. The principal testified that the moment he saw Beussink's homepage, he knew he was going to discipline him.

U.S. District Court Judge Rodney Sippel analyzed the case under the *Tinker* standard. According to Sippel, school officials "must be able to show that its action was caused by something more than a mere desire to avoid the discomfort and unpleasantness that always accompany an unpopular viewpoint." The judge relied on the principal's testimony that he disciplined Beussink because he was upset by the page's content, not because the home page had caused any substantial disruption at school. "Disliking or being upset by the content of a student's speech is not an acceptable justification for limiting student speech under *Tinker*," he wrote.[90] Judge Sippel concluded: "The public interest is not only served by allowing Beussink's message to be free from censure, but also by giving the students at Woodland High School this opportunity to see the protections of the United States Constitution and the Bill of Rights at work."[91]

In 2000, high school honors student Nick Emmett of Kent, Washington, created a home page that contained mock obituaries of two of his friends. The Web site became the big topic of discussion at school, and apparently someone started a rumor that the site contained a hit list. Emmett was suspended for harassment, intimidation, disruption of the educational environment and other violations.[92]

Emmett sued in federal court, arguing that his First Amendment rights were violated. In *Emmett v. Kent School District*, the judge noted that the Web site was created at home and not as part of any class project. The judge at one point appeared to apply *Tinker* by focusing on the fact that school officials failed to present any evidence that the obituaries or any other material on the Web site were intended to threaten anyone "or manifested any violent tendencies." At another point, however, the judge seemed to suggest that the case was simply beyond the power of school authorities to regulate at all: "Although the intended audience was undoubtedly connected to Kentlake High School, the speech was entirely outside of the school's supervision or control."[93]

These cases establish the principle that school officials violate the First Amendment when they punish students for blogging off campus. Even if a court determines that school officials have jurisdiction, many school officials will not be able to meet the *Tinker* standard and show any evidence of any disruption.

Summary

The difficult times public school students face are exacerbated by school administrators' post-Columbine consciousness and fear of the Internet. Columbine has led to a dramatic reduction in student constitutional rights.[94] These factors combine to allow the censorship of public school students who offer critical, offensive commentary on their own computers on their own

Web sites. School officials have a monumentally difficult and challenging task to ensure safety in a sometimes violent world. But they must make sure that they do not sacrifice student constitutional rights for the understandable goal of providing a safe learning environment.

The Internet offers an outlet for students who feel alienated at school. The Internet may even afford officials an opportunity to examine the potential dangerousness of certain disturbed students. The unparalleled educational opportunities of the Internet are often subsumed by talk about the pitfalls of cyberspace. School officials should avoid demonizing the Internet and try to use censorship controversies as teaching moments. It is hard for students to understand their constitutional rights and our constitutional democracy if they live day to day in an environment that does not respect them as citizens deserving of basic individual freedoms.

The First Amendment exists to allow people to offer dissenting opinions. Students are citizens who should also enjoy the protections of the Bill of Rights, particularly when they are in the privacy of their own homes. "We must be eternally vigilant to ensure that our fear of new technology and paranoia over school safety does not lead to a shedding of students' constitutional rights not only at the schoolhouse gate, but at their own computer."[95]

School Officials Should Have Broad Leeway to Regulate Student Blogs and Student Online Speech

I n 2005, a Florida teenager killed himself after facing repeated bullying online from another student. The boy's mother, Debbie Johnson, now campaigns vigorously for states to adopt so-called cyber-bullying laws designed to protect children and others from online harassment. "I'm here to draw the connection between bullying and teen suicide."[96] She has even petitioned and spoken with state legislators.

A 13-year-old boy in Essex Junction, Vermont, killed himself after being repeatedly taunted and bullied online by classmates. Several classmates sent him instant messages calling him gay and mocking him. In 2003, the boy killed himself. His father said the boy couldn't take it anymore.[97] Other students have faced severe emotional distress after reading horrible things written about them by fellow students online. Sometimes, students have written blogs that ridicule the 10 students they dislike the most or the 10 ugliest kids in school. In these instances, student blogging turns into a dangerous weapon, harming other children and even teachers and principals.

The weapon of online taunting is exacerbated by the power of the technology in terms of distribution and anonymity. The Internet transformed what was traditionally a confined, real-world event of bully-picking-on-victim to taunts that can be read by millions worldwide. Also, the Internet allows some harassers to make their comments anonymous, delivering their vicious assaults in secret.

The paramount duty of school officials is to provide a safe learning environment for their students. Unfortunately, in this day and age, violence remains a pervasive concern. The April 1999 shooting at Columbine High School in Littleton, Colorado, seared the soul of our collective conscience and showed that school violence was an awful reality. Sadly, Columbine is not alone, as school shootings have occurred in many places, such as Springfield, Oregon; Paducah, Kentucky; Jonesboro, Arkansas; Fayetteville, Tennessee; and Santee, California. The reality is that the country has entered a new day and age in schools, called by some the "age of Columbine."[98]

School violence does not just involve the extreme cases of shootings. Bullying has been an enduring problem in many schools. Much bullying surfaces on the Internet, as students post offensive comments, pictures of fights, and even hit lists online. School officials have responded by punishing students for harmful online material that negatively impacts other students, teachers, and principals. Legislators have responded in several states by passing laws against cyber-bullying, which criminalize online harassing and intimidation. Critics may cry out that these actions infringe on First Amendment rights to free speech, but much of the material on student blogs is the modern-day equivalent to what Justice Oliver Wendell Holmes termed in 1919 as "falsely shouting fire in a theatre and causing a panic."[99]

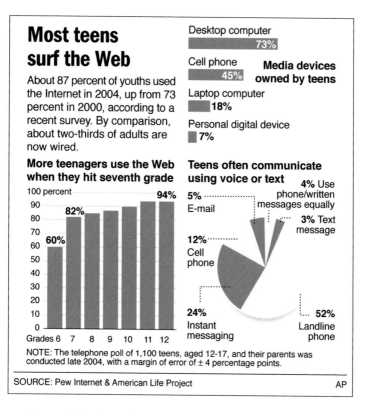

Most teens surf the Web

About 87 percent of youths used the Internet in 2004, up from 73 percent in 2000, according to a recent survey. By comparison, about two-thirds of adults are now wired.

Media devices owned by teens

Desktop computer 73%
Cell phone 45%
Laptop computer 18%
Personal digital device 7%

More teenagers use the Web when they hit seventh grade

100 percent
94%
82%
60%

Grades 6 7 8 9 10 11 12

Teens often communicate using voice or text

4% Use phone/written messages equally
5% E-mail
3% Text message
12% Cell phone
24% Instant messaging
52% Landline phone

NOTE: The telephone poll of 1,100 teens, aged 12-17, and their parents was conducted late 2004, with a margin of error of ± 4 percentage points.

SOURCE: Pew Internet & American Life Project   AP

The graphic above shows several different charts regarding the ways teens access information: by computer, cell phone, and other personal digital devices. The number of teenagers using the Internet rose between 2000 and 2004, from 73 percent to 87 percent.

The issue of student online expression is vital to school safety and discipline, given the sheer number of students who create online content. A November 2005 report by the PEW Internet and American Life Project found that 57 percent of students create online content.[100] The study showed that 19 percent of teens create their own blogs and nearly 40 percent read them. The number is probably much higher now.

Other student material posted online on blogs may not cause violence, but it disrupts the learning environment. The purpose of school is learning, the process of educating young minds. Students do not have any legal right to disrupt the school environment with their online ranting.

School officials need to monitor student blogs to ensure safety, learning, and discipline.

More and more schools have amended their student codes of conduct to include online postings. For example, Libertyville-Vernon Hills Area High School District 128 in northern Illinois

Arapahoe High School's Blogging Policy: "Safe and Responsible Blogging"

The most basic guideline to remember when blogging is that the blog is an extension of your classroom. You should not write anything on a blog that you would not say or write in your classroom. Use common sense, but if you are ever in doubt ask a teacher or parent whether or not what you are considering posting is appropriate. If you are going to err, err on the safe side. Here are some specific items to consider:

1. The use of blogs is considered an extension of your classroom. Therefore, any speech that is considered inappropriate in the classroom is inappropriate on a blog. This includes, but is not limited to, profanity; racist, sexist or discriminatory remarks; personal attacks.

2. Blogs are used primarily as learning tools, either as extensions of conversations and thinking outside of regular class time, or as the basis for beginning new classroom discussions. Either way, be sure to follow all rules and suggestions that are offered by your teachers regarding appropriate posting in your class.

3. Blogs are about ideas—therefore, agree or disagree with the idea, not the person. Freedom of speech does not give you the right to be uncivil. Use constructive criticism and use evidence to support your position. Read others' posts carefully—often in the heat of the moment you may think that a person is saying one thing, when really they are not. . . .

Source: Arapahoe High School, Arapahoe Blogging Policy. http://arapahoe.littletonpublic schools.net. Listed under Curriculum: Blogging Guidelines.

voted in May 2006 to amend the student code of conduct to cover online postings. "We want students to be aware that as they move into their adult lives, they are accountable for information that they put . . . out there on a blog site," said assistant superintendent Prentice Lea.[101]

Cyber-bullying is a serious problem that school officials must address.

No one disputes that students can enhance their educational experience through the Internet and, specifically, blogging. Students, teachers, and parents can communicate more quickly and efficiently through this online medium. But the Internet amplifies all types of expression, including harmful expression. Students have been harassed, ridiculed, and intimidated online. The phenomenon of cyber-bullying is a very real problem. Sometimes students will post threatening or bullying comments on their personal blog, and these comments will often harm other students by causing emotional distress and insecurity.

According to the National Conference of State Legislatures, 29 states have passed anti-bullying laws.[102] Many of these laws require school districts to adopt policies prohibiting harassment, intimidation, or bullying.[103] Several states have passed or are considering legislation designed to specifically address the problems of cyber-bullying. South Carolina and Idaho have already passed such a law, while similar measures have been introduced in Arkansas, New Jersey, Oregon, and Rhode Island.[104]

Schools should have the authority to regulate student blogging created off-campus that negatively affects the school environment.

Schools should develop an Internet-use policy that comments on the dangers of student blogging. Students must understand that they do not have the right to harass other students. Just because the harassment or ridicule or intimidation occurs online does not mean that it is acceptable or free from regulation.

Some courts have recognized in student Internet speech cases that school authority extends even to off-campus student expression. These courts have ruled that students can be punished for off-campus online expression if their material causes a disruption of school activities or invades the rights of other students and school personnel.[105] Additionally, courts

---

THE LETTER OF THE LAW

Idaho State Law Prohibiting Cyber-bullying

Idaho Code § 18-917A. Student harassment – Intimidation – Bullying
  (1) No student shall intentionally commit, or conspire to commit, an act of harassment, intimidation or bullying against another student.
  (2) As used in this section, "harassment, intimidation or bullying" means any intentional gesture, or any intentional written, verbal or physical act or threat by a student that:
     (a) A reasonable person under the circumstances should know will have the effect of:
        (i)   Harming a student; or
        (ii) Damaging a student's property; or
        (iii) Placing a student in reasonable fear of harm to his or her person; or
        (iv) Placing a student in reasonable fear of damage to his or her property; or
     (b) Is sufficiently severe, persistent or pervasive that it creates an intimidating, threatening or abusive educational environment for a student.
        An act of harassment, intimidation or bullying may also be committed through the use of a land line, car phone or wireless telephone or through the use of data or computer software that is accessed through a computer, computer system, or computer network.
  (3) A student who personally violates any provision of this section may be guilty of an infraction.

Source: Idaho Code § 18-917A.

have noted that student online expression can fall under school officials' jurisdiction if the intended audience is the school community. The Pennsylvania Supreme Court ruled in a 2002 decision that the fact that a Web site "was aimed not at a random audience, but at the specific audience of students and others connected with this particular School District" gave the school officials jurisdiction to punish the student.[106] The reasoning of this decision means that even if a student blogs from off campus, if the blog is intended to reach fellow students, it gives school officials jurisdiction to regulate the harmful effects of such expression.

THE LETTER OF THE LAW

South Carolina State Law Prohibiting Cyber-bullying

S.C. Code Ann. § 59-63-120 (2006)

As used in this article:

(1) "Harassment, intimidation, or bullying" means a gesture, **an electronic communication**, or a written, verbal, physical, or sexual act that is reasonably perceived to have the effect of:

   (a) harming a student physically or emotionally or damaging a student's property, or placing a student in reasonable fear of personal harm or property damage; or

   (b) insulting or demeaning a student or group of students causing substantial disruption in, or substantial interference with, the orderly operation of the school.

(2) "School" means in a classroom, on school premises, on a school bus or other school-related vehicle, at an official school bus stop, at a school-sponsored activity or event whether or not it is held on school premises, or at another program or function where the school is responsible for the child.

Source: S.C. Code Ann. § 59-63-120 (2006).

Unrestrained student blogging can lead to defamation lawsuits.

Online harassment, bullying, and intimidation is the not the only problem arising from student blogging and Web site ranting. Many students do not realize that they can be sued for defamation for false statements that they make about others. Defamation—often referred to as slander or libel—is a civil cause of action in which one person makes a false statement of fact about another that harms the subject's reputation. Across the country, teachers and administrators have filed defamation lawsuits against students after being victimized on the Internet.

In San Antonio, Texas, school principal Anna Draker filed a defamation action against two students after they went on

Legislation Under Consideration: Arkansas HB 1072

Whereas, cyberbullying, or the use of computers, websites, the Internet, cell phones, text messaging, chat rooms, and instating messaging to ridicule, harass, intimidate, humiliate, or otherwise bully another student, is a growing problem for public school students due to the increased use of such electronic devices by children both on and off of public school premises; and

Whereas, cyberbullies feel protected by anonymity and by the knowledge that children who are targeted do not want to report cyber assaults because they fear losing their access to electronic devices or having the situation aggravated by adult interference; and

Whereas, because cyberbullying has the potential for instantaneous distribution to a wide audience, it can impact the educational environment by rapidly reaching a large number of students and public school employees, and creating an environment of fear and intimidation that materially or substantially disrupts class work and discipline in a public school....

Source: Arkansas HB 1072.

MySpace.com, pretending to be Draker, and set up a site that made false statements about her sexual orientation and other private matters. Draker's attorney referred to the student-generated comments as "four pages of filth."[107] Her attorney says that her client filed the suit in part because school officials felt they may not have jurisdiction to discipline the students for off-campus conduct.

Unfortunately, the Anna Draker lawsuit is not alone. In Minnesota, an eighth-grader allegedly created a fake MySpace page that depicted one of his teachers as a child pornographer.[108] A similar incident occurred in Farmington, Connecticut, where a 13-year-old girl allegedly created a bogus Web site, pretending to be her teacher. The girl then posted inappropriate comments about other students.[109] A student in Indiana had to pay monetary damages to three teachers whom he defamed on his personal Web site. A teacher in Orlando, Florida, sued after a student posted demeaning sexual comments about the teacher online.[110]

Students take a very real legal risk when they go online and post false statements about teachers, administrators, and fellow students. They exacerbate those risks when they commit fraud by posing as someone else when making comments. Students need to be aware that there are often very serious legal consequences to such actions. Schools must subject students to codes of conduct that establish the limits of student blogging. Such policies may help students learn that with rights come responsibilities.

Summary

Schools are going through a period called the "Age of Columbine," an age in which school violence remains an awful reality. In this day and time, however, violence means far more than occasional school shootings. Violence occurs not only through the occasional firing of guns, but also through the much more frequent firing of verbal assaults on the Internet. Cyber-bullying has become a very real problem in schools, with students sometimes causing grave harm to classmates with vicious online assaults. Schools must be given broad leeway to address this growing problem. In the words of legal commentator Renee Servance, "Courts need to allow schools to address these new concerns without fear of liability under the First Amendment."[111]

Students must realize that the Internet and the power of blogging do provide great educational opportunities. They improve communication and can make learning easier and more interesting. But there are dangers with these advancements. Students must realize that there are very real legal consequences when they attack people online. The First Amendment does not protect threats. Students need to realize that school blogging policies are put in place to help students comply with existing laws. Students must learn that when they post things on the Internet, their comments are there for others—including potential future employers and college administrators—to see. There are real-world repercussions for negative online speech.

Controversies Over the Blogosphere Are Here to Stay

The liberty of the press is not confined to newspapers and periodicals. It necessarily embraces pamphlets and leaflets. These indeed have been historic weapons in the defense of liberty, as the pamphlets of Thomas Paine and others in our own history abundantly attest. The press in its connotation comprehends every sort of publication which affords a vehicle of information and opinion. What we have had recent occasion to say with respect to the vital importance of protecting this essential liberty from every sort of infringement need not be repeated.

—U.S. Supreme Court Chief Justice Charles E. Hughes[112]

The exponential expansion of the blogosphere assures that controversies regarding blogging will be with us for much of the twenty-first century. The three issues emphasized in this book represent only some of the more high-profile controversies. There are others. They include how existing campaign finance laws apply to bloggers,[113] how law blogs impact the legal profession,[114] and how employee blogging coexists with trade secret laws.[115] Another issue concerns whether existing libel laws should be modified in some capacity in the blogosphere.

Perhaps the most pressing issue for the courts has been how to balance the First Amendment right to blog anonymously on the Internet against the right of individuals to protect the value

FROM THE BENCH

Talley v. California, 362 U.S. 60, 64–65 (1960)

Anonymous pamphlets, leaflets, brochures and even books have played an important role in the progress of mankind. Persecuted groups and sects from time to time throughout history have been able to criticize oppressive practices and laws either anonymously or not at all. The obnoxious press licensing law of England, which was also enforced on the Colonies was due in part to the knowledge that exposure of the names of printers, writers and distributors would lessen the circulation of literature critical of the government. The old seditious libel cases in England show the lengths to which government had to go to find out who was responsible for books that were obnoxious to the rulers. John Lilburne was whipped, pilloried and fined for refusing to answer questions designed to get evidence to convict him or someone else for the secret distribution of books in England. Two Puritan Ministers, John Penry and John Udal, were sentenced to death on charges that they were responsible for writing, printing or publishing books. Before the Revolutionary War colonial patriots frequently had to conceal their authorship or distribution of literature that easily could have brought down on them prosecutions by English-controlled courts. Along about that time the Letters of Junius were written and the identity of their author is unknown to this day. Even the Federalist Papers, written in favor of the adoption of our Constitution, were published under fictitious names. It is plain that anonymity has sometimes been assumed for the most constructive purposes.

Source: *Talley v. California*, 362 U.S. 60, 64–65 (1960).

of their good name. The U.S. Supreme Court has made clear that anonymous speech deserves First Amendment protection. In *Talley v. California*, the court wrote: "Anonymous pamphlets, leaflets, brochures, and even books have played an important role in the progress of mankind."[116]

Several of the founders of the United States published historic political articles anonymously. James Madison, John Jay, and Alexander Hamilton wrote the 85 essays in the *Federalist Papers* under the pen name "Publius." These anonymous essays are now lauded as among the foundational writings of their time. The U.S. Supreme Court noted in an anonymous-speech case more recently: "Anonymous pampleteering is not a pernicious, fraudulent practice, but an honorable tradition of advocacy and of dissent."[117]

Some individuals who post anonymous messages criticize employers, government officials, and others. Sometimes it is valid criticism and other times it could be vile defamation. Online libel remains a real risk for those who blog, as it does for any writer or reporter in any medium. Because of this, "The question becomes, how does the legal system protect the First Amendment–based right to anonymous speech while still affording a remedy to individuals whose reputations have been trashed unfairly online."[118]

Some employers have resorted to filing defamation lawsuits simply to silence critical speech. Some of these suits resemble so-called SLAPP suits—Strategic Lawsuits Against Public Participation. These frivolous lawsuits seek to silence an online critic by unmasking them and then retaliating against them. But companies and individuals do file legitimate libel suits, as well, seeking to uncover the identity of the intemperate flamethrower.[119]

"It is essential that bloggers can participate in the public discourse without fear that someone can file a meritless lawsuit and then use the power of the courts to discover their identities," says Kurt Opsahl. "The possibility that a frivolous claim could pierce the veil of anonymity might silence a blogger and remove

Above, bloggers attend a conference to learn techniques used by mainstream journalists. There has been some controversy over whether news-reporting bloggers are journalists and whether they should receive the same protections granted to the press.

a valuable voice from the debate. Accordingly, a plaintiff must be held to a strict standard, and first produce sufficient evidence to support each element of its cause of action."[120]

The courts have come up with different legal standards in determining when a libel plaintiff can unmask an anonymous blogger. In September 2005, the Delaware Supreme Court set a high standard for identity disclosure in *Cahill v. Doe.*[121] In this case, a Smyrna, Delaware, city council official named Patrick Cahill sued a John Doe for defamation after this unknown blogger made numerous negative statements about the council member, including questioning his competence, paranoia, and mental makeup. The writer of these comments was known only as "Proud Citizen." Cahill wanted to uncover the identity of his online attacker. The Delaware high court wrote that "before a defamation plaintiff can obtain the identity of an anonymous defendant through the compulsory discovery process, he must support his defamation claim with facts sufficient to defeat a summary judgment motion."[122] This standard means that before the libel plaintiff can discover the identity of the defendant blogger, the plaintiff must show that he can arguably establish the essential elements of the libel claim. The court set this high standard to ensure that plaintiffs would not file suits simply to discover the identity of the person and then retaliate against them in some capacity.

The public official argued that the Delaware high court should adopt, as the lower court had, a lower standard, such as the good-faith standard. This standard simply means that the plaintiff has a reasonable good-faith belief that the suit is valid. The state high court would not adopt that lower standard, however, writing that "allowing a defamation plaintiff to unmask an anonymous defendant's identity through the judicial process is a crucial form of relief that, if too easily obtained, will chill the exercise of First Amendment rights to free speech."

Some courts, however, have applied the lower good-faith standard, which essentially allows the uncovering of an online poster if the defamation plaintiff had a reasonable belief that the suit was valid. In other words, the good-faith standard would make it easy for a defamation plaintiff to unmask an anonymous critic. While the good-faith standard would help those filing defamation actions, it might hinder the development of freedom of speech on the Internet.

"I rather like the summary judgment standard from the Delaware Supreme Court in *Cahill v. Doe*," says free-speech

FROM THE BENCH

Doe v. Cahill, 844 A.2d 451, 457 (2005)

We are concerned that setting the standard too low will chill potential posters from exercising their First Amendment right to speak anonymously. The possibility of losing anonymity in a future lawsuit could intimidate anonymous posters into self-censoring their comments or simply not commenting at all. A defamation plaintiff, particularly a public figure, obtains a very important form of relief by unmasking the identity of his anonymous critics. The revelation of identity of an anonymous speaker "may subject [that speaker] to ostracism for expressing unpopular ideas, invite retaliation from those who oppose her ideas or from those whom she criticizes, or simply give unwanted exposure to her mental processes." Plaintiffs can often initially plead sufficient facts to meet the good faith test applied by the Superior Court, even if the defamation claim is not very strong, or worse, if they do not intend to pursue the defamation action to a final decision. After obtaining the identity of an anonymous critic through the compulsory discovery process, a defamation plaintiff who either loses on the merits or fails to pursue a lawsuit is still free to engage in extra-judicial self-help remedies; more bluntly, the plaintiff can simply seek revenge or retribution.

Indeed, there is reason to believe that many defamation plaintiffs bring suit merely to unmask the identities of anonymous critics. As one commentator has noted, "the sudden surge in John Doe suits stems from the fact that many defamation actions are not really about money." "The goals of this new breed of libel action are largely symbolic, the primary goal being to silence John Doe and others like him." This "sue first, ask questions later" approach, coupled with a standard only minimally protective of the anonymity of defendants, will discourage debate on important issues of public concern as more and more anonymous posters censor their online statements in response to the likelihood of being unmasked.

Source: *Doe v. Cahill*, 844 A.2d 451, 457 (2005).

expert Robert O'Neil. "I am comfortable with setting a high standard given the value and interest in anonymous speech on the Internet."[123]

O'Neil gave several reasons for favoring a high standard for the disclosure of online identity. "First, those who post anonymous communications perhaps naively but in reasonably good faith assume they will have substantial protection of their identity," he said, continuing:

> Second, in an electronic world, there are fewer alternatives or equivalents to the various forms of communication in a print world. In the online world you are either identified or not unmasked and there is nothing in between. There is nothing like printing posters or hiring someone to post them up for you in the online world. Some of the great promise of the Internet as a democratizing, speech-enhancing medium does depend on some level of protection for the anonymous critic. . . .[124]

The summary judgment standard is superior to many free-speech experts, because it makes it more likely than an anonymous Internet speaker can remain unknown and not have their speech rights chilled on the Internet. A defamation plaintiff can still unmask anonymous online vandals, but only if they really establish that their lawsuit is a meritorious one.

Summary

Blogging represents a worldwide phenomenon that has its opponents and proponents. Blogs can inform, educate, titillate, inflame, and enrage. Nearly every segment of the public blogosphere—students, employees, and journalists—raises important legal and societal issues and controversies. Even politicians have made use of the medium to communicate with their constituents and campaign for office. Blogging is a revolutionary medium of communication because it enables an average person to communicate to a wide audience at relatively low cost. In the words of professor Donald Kochan: "Traditional media is no longer fully in charge of information flow. The blogosphere allows anyone to be a publisher, anyone to be an author, anyone to have their own imprint, and anyone to have their own broadcast."[125]

Introduction: Blogging

1 *American Civil Liberties Union v. Reno*, 929 F. Supp. 824, 882–883 (E.D. Pa. 1996).

2 Jonathan Yang, *The Rough Guide to Blogging* (New York: Rough Guides Ltd., 2006), pp. 4–5.

3 *Ibid.*, 5.

4 *Ibid.*

5 *Ibid.*

6 *Ibid.*, 4.

7 Tom Goldstein, in discussion with the author, May 2007.

8 David L. Hudson Jr., *Student Expression in the Age of Columbine: Securing Safety and Protecting First Amendment Rights* (Nashville, Tenn: First Amendment Center, 2005), p. 1.

9 Amanda Lenhert and Susannah Fox, "Bloggers: A Portrait of the Internet's New Storytellers." Pew Internet and American Life Report, July 2006. http://www.pewinternet.org/pdfs/PIP%20Bloggers%20Report%20July%2019%202006.pdf.

Point: Many Bloggers Are Journalists Who Deserve the Protection of a Reporter Shield Law

10 Quoted in David L. Hudson Jr., "Blogging and the First Amendment," First Amendment Center Online. http://www.firstamendmentcenter.org/Press/topic.aspx?topic=blogging.

11 Mary-Rose Papandrea, "Citizen Journalism and the Reporter's Privilege," 91 *Minnesota Law Review* 515, p. 24 (2007).

12 408 U.S. 665 (1972).

13 *Ibid.*, 703–704.

14 *Ibid.*, 725 (J. Stewart, dissenting).

15 *Ibid.*, 743 (J. Stewart, dissenting).

16 "*U.S. v. Wolf*" at the home page of Josh Wolf. http://www.joshwolf.net/freejosh/?page_id=17.

17 Kim Pearson, "Josh Wolf: Video Blogger at the Center of Controversy Over Journalists' Rights," *USC Annenburg Online*

Journalism Review, Oct. 3, 2006. http://www.ojr.org/ojr/stories/061002pearson.

18 S. 1267 (110th Congress), Section 4.

19 *O'Grady v. The Superior Court of Santa Clara County*, 139 Cal. App. 4th 1423 (2006).

20 *Ibid.*, 1459.

21 *Ibid.*, 1462.

22 Quoted in Hudson, "Blogging and the First Amendment"

23 Kurt Opsahl, in discussion with the author, November 2005.

24 Robert Cox, in discussion with the author, November 2005.

25 Christopher B. Daly, "Are Bloggers Journalists? Let's Ask Thomas Jefferson." http://www.bu.edu/cdaly/whoisajournalist.html.

26 *Ibid.*

Counterpoint: Bloggers Should Not Receive the Protections of Mainstream Journalists

27 *Lee v. Department of Justice*, 401 F.Supp. 2d 123, 140 (D.D.C. 2005).

28 John Seigenthaler, "A false Wikipedia biography," *USA TODAY*, Nov. 29, 2005. http://www.usatoday.com/news/opinion/editorials/2005-11-29-wikipedia-edit_x.htm.

29 Ralph Loos, "Wary of Wikipedia: Global Search Engine's Accuracy Questioned," *Tennessean*, Feb. 18, 2007, B1.

30 *Ibid.*

31 *Branzburg v. Hayes*, 408 U.S. 665 (1972).

32 *Ibid.*, 704.

33 *Ibid.*

34 *In Re Grand Jury Subpoena* (Judith Miller), 397 F.3d 964, 979–980 (D.C. Cir. 2005) (J. Sentelle, concurring).

35 Ala. Code § 12-21-142.

36 A.R.S. § 12-2237.

37 Ark. Code Ann. § 16-85-510.

38 Sen. Patrick Leahy, speaking to the Senate Judiciary Committee, on Oct. 19, 2005. http://judiciary.senate.gov/member_statement.cfm?id=1637&wit_id=2629.

39 Quoted in David L. Hudson Jr., "Blogs and the First Amendment," 11 *Nexus Journal* 129, 131 (2006).

40 David Shaw, "Media Matters: Do bloggers deserve basic journalistic protections?" *Los Angeles Times*, (March 27, 2005): p. E14.

41 *Ibid.*

42 Fernanda Viegas, "Bloggers' Expectations of Privacy and Accountability: An Initial Survey," *Journal of Computer-Mediated Communication* 10 (2005). http://jcmc .indiana.edu/vol10/issue3/viegas.html.

Point: Employees Should Have the Right to Blog Without Fear of Reprisal From Employers

43 Amy Joyce, "Free Expression Can Be Costly When Bloggers Bad-Mouth Jobs," *Washington Post*, Feb. 11, 2005. http:// www.washingtonpost.com/wp-dyn/ articles/A15511-2005Feb10.html.

44 Joyce, "Free Expression Can Be Costly When Bloggers Bad-Mouth Jobs."

45 Ellen Simonetti, in discussion with the author, May 2007.

46 Stephanie Armour, "Warning: Your Clever Little Blog Could Get You Fired," *USA Today*, June 15, 2005, B1.

47 *McAuliffe v. New Bedford*, 155 Mass. 216, 29 N.E. 517 (1892).

48 Hudson, "Teacher Looks Back on Letter that Led to Firing—and Supreme Court Victory," First Amendment Center Online. July 20, 2001. http://www .firstamendmentcenter.org/analysis .aspx?id=4828.

49 *Ibid.*

50 *Pickering v. Board of Education*, 391 U.S. 563, 568 (1968).

51 Ibid., 572.

52 Henry Hoang Pham, "Bloggers and the Workplace: The Search for a Legal Solution To the Conflict Between Employee Blogging and Employers," 26 *Loyola Entertainment Law Review* 207 (2006): p. 212–213.

53 Robert Sprague, "Fired for Blogging: Are There Legal Protections for Employees Who Blog?" 9 *University of Pennsylvania*

Journal of Labor & Employment Law 355 (2007): p. 387.

54 *Payne v. Western & Atlantic Railroad*, 81 Tenn. 507 (1884): pp. 519–520.

55 Steven D. Lichtenstein and Jonathan J. Darrow, "Employment Termination for Employee Blogging: Number One Tech Trend for 2005 and Beyond, or a Recipe for Getting Dooced?" *UCLA Journal of Law & Technology* (2004): p. 4.

56 Hudson, "Blogs and the First Amendment," p. 134.

57 Katherine M. Scott, "When Is Employee Blogging Protected by Section 7 of the NLRA?" *Duke Law & Technology Journal* (2006) 0017. http://www.law.duke.edu/ journals/dltr/articles/2006DLTR0017 .html.

Counterpoint: Employers Should Have Wide Latitude to Discipline Bloggers for Comments Detrimental to the Workplace

58 Paul S. Gutman, "Say What? Blogging and Employment Law in Conflict," *Columbia Journal of Law & Arts* 27 (2003): pp. 145, 150–151.

59 Lichtenstein and Darrow, "Employment Termination for Employee Blogging," paragraph no. 68.

60 Gutman, "Say What?" p. 151.

61 *Ibid.*

62 Lichtenstein and Darrow, "Employment Termination for Employee Blogging," at paragraph 71.

63 Konrad Lee, "Anti-Employer Blogging: Employee Breach of the Duty of Loyalty and the Procedure for Allowing Discovery of a Blogger's Identity before Service of Process is Effected," *Duke Law & Technology* 2 (2006): paragraph no. 1.

64 Quoted in Joyce, "Free Expression Can Be Costly When Bloggers Bad-Mouth Jobs."

65 *Marsh v. Delta Air Lines, Inc.*, 952 F. Supp. 1458 (D. Colo. 1997).

66 Ibid., 1463.

67 *Pickering v. Board of Education*, 391 U.S. 563, 569–570 (1968).

68 *Buazard v. Meredith*, 172 F. 3d 546, 548 (8th Cir. 1999).

69 Hudson, "Balancing Act: Public Employees and Free Speech," First Amendment Center, December 2002. http://www.firstamendmentcenter.org/about.aspx?id=6423, p. 26.

70 *Connick v. Myers*, 461 U.S. 138, 151–152 (1983).

71 *Pereira v. Commission of Social Services*, 733 N.E.2d 112 (Mass. 2000).

72 *Ibid.*, 122.

73 Quoted in Hudson, "Blogging and the First Amendment."

74 Dan Cordtz, "Employee Blogs That Trash Others Can Be Actionable," *The Recorder* (July 26, 2005).

Point: School Officials Don't Have Authority to Regulate Students' Off-Campus Blogging

75 Kenneth A. Paulson, "Long Arm of Censors Shouldn't Reach Student Homes." First Amendment Center Online, April 30, 1998. http://www.freedomforum.org/templates/document.asp?documentID=6577.

76 *Lavine v. Blaine School District*, 279 F.3d 719, 729 (J. Kleinfeld, dissenting from denial of certiorari).

77 Maudlyne Ihejirika, "Blog Gets 3 Students in Trouble," *Chicago Sun-Times*, (Dec. 8, 2005): p. A3.

78 *Ibid.*

79 "Student Suspended for MySpace Postings Returns to School," First Amendment Center Online, Feb. 22, 2006. http://www.firstamendmentcenter.org/news.aspx?id=16526.

80 *Reno v. ACLU*, 521 U.S. 844 (1997).

81 Hudson, "First Amendment Triumphs Mark Attorney's Supreme Court Record." First Amendment Center Online, Sept. 25, 1998. http://www.firstamendmentcenter.org/news.aspx?id=8583.

82 Quoted in Hudson, "Student Online Expression: What Do the Internet and MySpace Mean for Students' First Amendment Rights?" First Amendment Center Online, First Forum, 2006. http://www.firstamendmentcenter.org/PDF/student.internet.speech.pdf. [PDF]

83 *Klein v. Smith*, 635 F.Supp. 1440 (D. Me. 1986).

84 Quoted in Hudson, *The Silencing of Student Voices: Preserving Free Speech in America's Schools* (Nashville, Tenn: First Amendment Center, 2003): p. 55.

85 *Ibid.*

86 *Tinker v. Des Moines Comm. Sch. Dist.*, 393 U.S. 503 (1969).

87 *Ibid.*, 506.

88 *Ibid.*, 508.

89 *Beussink v. Wooland R-IV Sch. Dist.*, 30 F.Supp. 2d 1175 (E.D. Mo. 1998).

90 *Ibid.*, 1180.

91 *Ibid.*, 1182.

92 *Emmett v. Kent Sch. Dist.*, 92 F.Supp. 2d 1088 (W.D. Wash. 2000).

93 *Ibid.*, 1090.

94 Hudson, *Student Expression in the Age of Columbine*, xx.

95 Hudson, "Censorship of Student Internet Speech: The Effect of Diminishing Student Rights, Fear of the Internet and Columbine." 2000 M.S.U.-D.C.L. 199. http://www.law.msu.edu/lawrev/2000-1/Hudson.htm and http://www.freedomforum.org/templates/document.asp?documentID=14592.

Counterpoint: School Officials Should Have Broad Leeway to Regulate Student Blogs and Student Online Speech

96 Larry Wheeler, "Anti-Bullying Push: Cape Group Meets Congressman," *News-Press* (Fort Myers, Fla., Sept. 8, 2006): p. 1A.

97 Associated Press, "Some States Pushing for Laws to Curb Online Bullying," First Amendment Center Online, Feb. 11, 2007. http://www.firstamendmentcenter.org//news.aspx?id=18118.

98 Hudson, "Student Expression in the Age of Columbine." http://www.firstamendmentcenter.org/about.aspx?id=15858.

99 *Schenck v. United States*, 249 U.S. 47 (1919).

100 Amanda Lenhart and Mary Madden, "Teen Content Creators and Consumers."

PEW Internet and American Life Project, Nov. 2005, p. 1. http://www.pewinternet.org/pdfs/PIP_Teens_Content_Creation.pdf.

101 Quoted in Dean Reynolds, "Detention for a High School Blog Entry?" ABCNews.com, May 23, 2006, http://abcnews.go.com/WNT/story?id=1995856&page=1.

102 National Conference of State Legislators. "School Bullying Overview." http://www.ncsl.org/programs/educ/bullyingoverview.htm.

103 See, e.g., T.C.A. § 49-6-1016(a): "Each school district shall adopt a policy prohibiting harassment, intimidation or bullying. School districts are encouraged to develop the policy after consultation with parents and guardians, school employees, volunteers, students, administrators and community representatives."

104 Associated Press, "Some states pushing for laws to curb online bullying."

105 Hudson, "Student Online Expression," pp. 16–20.

106 *J.S. v. Bethlehem Area School District*, 807 A.2d 847, 865 (Pa. 2002).

107 Murphy Klasing, quoted in Hudson, "Student Online Expression," p. 27.

108 Associated Press, "8th-Grader Blamed For Teacher's Fake MySpace Page." April 22, 2006. http://wcco.com/topstories/local_story_112160715.html.

109 Associated Press, "Teen Accused of Posing as Teacher on MySpace." Oct. 24, 2006. http://www.foxnews.com/story/0,2933,224937,00.html?sPage=fnc.technology/personaltechnology.

110 Hudson, "Student Expression in the Age of Columbine," p. 27.

111 Renee Servance, "Cyberbullying, Cyber-Harassment, and the Conflict Between Schools and the First Amendment," 2003 *Wisconsin Law Review* (2003): pp. 1213, 1244.

Conclusion: Controversies Over the Blogosphere Are Here to Stay

112 *Lovell v. City of Griffin*, 303 U.S. 444, 452 (1938).

113 Richard Hasen, "Lessons from the Clash Between Campaign Finance Laws and the Blogosphere," 11 *Nexus Journal of Opinion* 23 (2006). http://www.nexusjournal.org/volume11/NEX103.pdf.

114 Denise Howell, "Blog You." 11 *Nexus Journal of Opinion* 69 (2006). http://www.nexusjournal.org/volume11/NEX106.pdf.

115 Vincent Chiappetta, "Employee Blogs and Trade Secrets: Legal Responses to Technological Change." 11 *Nexus Journal of Opinion* 31 (2006). http://www.nexusjournal.org/volume11/NEX104.pdf.

116 *Talley v. California*, 362 U.S. 60, 64 (1960).

117 *McIntryre v. Ohio Election Commission*, 514 U.S. 334, 357 (1995).

118 Hudson, "Blogging and the First Amendment."

119 *Ibid.*

120 *Ibid.*

121 *Cahill v. Doe*, 844 A.2d 451 (Del. 2005).

122 *Ibid.*, 460.

123 Quoted in Hudson, "Blogging and the First Amendment."

124 Ibid.

RESORURCES //////

Books and Articles

Armour, Stephanie. "Warning: Your Clever Little Blog Could Get You Fired." *USA Today*, June 15, 2005, B1.

Chiappetta, Vincent. "Employee Blogs and Trade Secrets: Legal Responses to Technological Change." 11 *Nexus Journal of Opinion* 31 (2006). Available online. URL: http://www.nexusjournal.org/volume11/NEX104.pdf. Accessed June 2, 2007.

Cordtz, Dan. "Employee Blogs That Trash Others Can Be Actionable." *The Recorder* (July 26, 2005).

Gutman, Paul S. "Say What? Blogging and Employment Law in Conflict." 27 *Columbia Journal of Law & Arts* 145 (2003).

Hasen, Richard L. "Lessons from the Clash Between Campaign Finance Laws and the Blogosphere." 11 *Nexus Journal of Opinion* 23 (2006). Available online. URL: http://www.nexusjournal.org/volume11/NEX103.pdf. Accessed June 2, 2007.

Howell, Denise. "Blog You." 11 *Nexus Journal of Opinion* 69 (2006). Available online. URL: http://www.nexusjournal.org/volume11/NEX106.pdf. Accessed June 2, 2007.

Hudson, David L., Jr. "Censorship of Student Internet Speech: The Effect of Diminishing Student Rights, Fear of the Internet and Columbine." 2000 M.S.U.-D.C.L. 199. Available online. URL: http://www.freedomforum.org/templates/document.asp?documentID=14592. Accessed June 3, 2007.

———. "Balancing Act: Public Employees and Free Speech." First Amendment Center (December 2002). Available online. URL: http://www.firstamendmentcenter.org/about.aspx?id=6423. Accessed June 2, 2007.

———. "Student Expression in the Age of Columbine: Securing Safety and Protecting First Amendment Rights." First Amendment Center (Sept. 2005). Available online. URL: http://www.firstamendmentcenter.org/about.aspx?id=17913. Accessed June 3, 2007.

———. "Blogs and the First Amendment." 11 *Nexus Journal* 129, 131 (2006).

Ihejirika, Maudlyne. "Blog Gets 3 Students in Trouble." *Chicago Sun-Times*, (Dec. 8, 2005): p. A3.

Joyce, Amy. "Free Expression Can Be Costly When Bloggers Bad-Mouth Jobs." *Washington Post* (Feb. 11, 2005). Available online. URL: http://www

.washingtonpost.com/ac2/wp-dyn/A15511-2005Feb10?language=printer. Accessed June 2, 2007.

Kochan, Donald J. "The Blogosphere and the New Pamphleteers." 11 *Nexus Journal of Opinion* 99 (2006). Available online. URL: http://www .nexusjournal.org/volume11/NEX110.pdf. Accessed June 3, 2007.

Lee, Konrad. "Anti-Employer Blogging: Employee Breach of the Duty of Loyalty and the Procedure for Allowing Discovery of a Blogger's Identity Before Service of Process is Effected." 2006 *Duke Law & Technology* 2.

Lenhert, Amanda, and Susannah Fox. "Bloggers: A Portrait of the Internet's New Storytellers." Pew Internet and American Life Report (July 2006). Available online. URL: http://www.pewinternet.org/pdfs/PIP%20Bloggers %20Report%20July%2019%202006.pdf. Accessed June 3, 2007.

Lenhart, Amanda, and Mary Madden. "Teen Content Creators and Consumers." PEW Internet and American Life Project (November 2005): p. 1. Available online. URL: http://www.pewinternet.org/pdfs/PIP_Teens _Content_Creation.pdf. Accessed June 3, 2007.

Lichtenstein, Steven D., and Jonathan J. Darrow. "Employment Termination for Employee Blogging: Number One Tech Trend for 2005 and Beyond, or a Recipe for Getting Dooced?" 2006 *UCLA Journal of Law & Technology* 4.

Papandrea, Mary-Rose. "Citizen Journalism and the Reporter's Privilege," 91 *Minnesota Law Review* 515 (2007): p.

Paulson, Kenneth A. "Long Arm of Censors Shouldn't Reach Student Homes." First Amendment Center Online (April 30, 1998). Available online. URL: http://www.freedomforum.org/templates/document .asp?documentID=6577. Accessed June 3, 2007.

Pearson, Kim. "Josh Wolf: Video Blogger at the Center of Controversy Over Journalists' Rights." *USC Annenburg Online Journalism Review* (Oct. 3, 2006). Available online. URL: http://www.ojr.org/ojr/stories/ 061002pearson.

Pham, Henry Hoang. "Bloggers and the Workplace: The Search for a Legal Solution To the Conflict Between Employee Blogging and Employers." 26 *Loyola Entertainment Law Review* 207 (2006).

Scott, Katherine M. "When Is Employee Blogging Protected by Section 7 of the NLRA?" 2006 *Duke Law & Technology Journal* 0017. Available online. URL: http://www.law.duke.edu/journals/dltr/articles/2006DLTR0017 .html. Accessed June 3, 2007.

Seigenthaler, John. "A False Wikipedia biography." *USA Today*, (Nov. 29, 2005). Available online. URL: http://www.usatoday.com/news/opinion/editorials/2005-11-29-wikipedia-edit_x.htm. Accessed June 3, 2007.

Servance, Renee. "Cyberbullying, Cyber-Harassment, and the Conflict Between Schools and the First Amendment." 2003 *Wisconsin Law Review* 1213 (2003).

Shaw, David. "Media Matters: Do Bloggers Deserve Basic Journalistic Protections?" *Los Angeles Times* (March 27, 2005): p. E14.

Sprague, Robert. "Fired for Blogging: Are There Legal Protections for Employees Who Blog?" 9 *University of Pennsylvania Journal of Labor & Employment Law* 355 (2007).

Viegas, Fernanda. "Bloggers' Expectations of Privacy and Accountability: An Initial Survey." *Journal of Computer-Mediated Communication* 10 (2005). Available online. URL: http://jcmc.indiana.edu/vol10/issue3/viegas.html. Accessed June 3, 2007.

Yang, Jonathan. *The Rough Guide to Blogging.* New York: Rough Guides Ltd., 2006.

Web sites

Bloggers Unite
www.bloggers-unite.com
This site provides support for bloggers for their sites.

Center for Citizen Media Blog
http://citmedia.org/blog
This blog promotes citizen journalism or grassroots journalism.

CyberJournalist
www.cyberjournalist.net
This informative site discusses a wide range of issues impacting bloggers.

How Appealing
http://howappealing.law.com
This blog, created by Philadelphia-based appellate attorney Howard Bashman, is one of the most popular law blogs.

InstaPundit
www.instapundit.com
This blog, created by Tennessee law professor Glenn Reynolds, is another popular legal blog.

Media Bloggers Association

www.mediabloggers.org/node
This blog advocates on behalf of many bloggers as journalists.

Talking Points Memo

www.talkingpointsmemo.com
This political blog, maintained by Joshua Micah Marshall, writes from a perspective on the left.

Technorati

http://technorati.com/pop/blogs
This site tracks the number of blogs and the most popular blogs in the world.

Cases

Bethel School District v. Fraser, 478 U.S. 675 (1986).
This U.S. Supreme Court decision ruled that public school officials can punish students for lewd and vulgar expression.

Beussink v. Woodland Community School District, 30 F. Supp. 2d 1175 (E.D. Mo. 1998).
This federal district court decision ruled that public school officials could not punish a student for the content of his off-campus created Web site simply because they did not like it.

Branzburg v. Hayes, 408 U.S. 665 (1972).
This U.S. Supreme Court established that journalists have no First Amendment right to withhold information from a valid grand jury subpoena even if they have promised confidentiality to their sources. The decision was sharply divided at 5 to 4, as Justice Potter Stewart's dissent provided the blueprint for many reporter shield laws passed after the court's decision.

In Re Grand Jury Subpoena (Judith Miller), 397 F.3d 964 (D.C. Cir. 2005).
This federal appeals court decision, involving former *New York Times* reporter Judith Miller, deals with the issue of reporter subpoenas and confidential sources. In a concurring opinion, Judge David Sentelle writes about whether any reporter privilege would be extended to bloggers.

Lee v. Department of Justice, 401 F. Supp. 2d 123 (D.D.C. 2005).
This is a recent federal court decision dealing with whether journalists have to comply with valid government subpoenas.

O'Grady v. The Superior Court of Santa Clara County, 139 Cal. App. 4th 1423 (2006).
This California appeals court decision provided that the state's reporter shield law was broad enough to cover bloggers. It remains to be seen how persuasive this decision will be for other courts.

Pickering v. Board of Education, 391 U.S. 563, 568 (1968).
This U.S. Supreme Court decision established that public employees do not lose all their First Amendment rights when they accept public employment.

Reno v. ACLU, 544 U.S. 821 (1997).
This U.S. Supreme Court decision established that speech on the Internet was entitled to the highest degree of First Amendment protection, akin to the print medium. The case involves a criminal law that sought to punish online purveyors of pornography. The court struck down provisions of the law as too vague.

Tinker v. Des Moines Independent Community School District, 393 U.S. 503 (1969).
This U.S. Supreme Court decision established that public school students have First Amendment rights at school. The court determined that public school

officials could censor student expression only if they could reasonably forecast that the student expression would cause a substantial disruption of school activities or would invade the rights of others.

Terms and Concepts

blog

citizen journalism

cyber-bullying

dooced

First Amendment

journalist

public concern

reporter shield law

subpoena

Beginning Legal Research

The goal of Point/Counterpoint is not only to provide the reader with an introduction to a controversial issue affecting society, but also to encourage the reader to explore the issue more fully. This appendix, then, is meant to serve as a guide to the reader in researching the current state of the law as well as exploring some of the public-policy arguments as to why existing laws should be changed or new laws are needed.

Like many types of research, legal research has become much faster and more accessible with the invention of the Internet. This appendix discusses some of the best starting points, but of course "surfing the Net" will uncover endless additional sources of information—some more reliable than others. Some important sources of law are not yet available on the Internet, but these can generally be found at the larger public and university libraries. Librarians usually are happy to point patrons in the right direction.

The most important source of law in the United States is the Constitution. Originally enacted in 1787, the Constitution outlines the structure of our federal government and sets limits on the types of laws that the federal government and state governments can pass. Through the centuries, a number of amendments have been added to or changed in the Constitution, most notably the first ten amendments, known collectively as the Bill of Rights, which guarantee important civil liberties. Each state also has its own constitution, many of which are similar to the U.S. Constitution. It is important to be familiar with the U.S. Constitution because so many of our laws are affected by its requirements. State constitutions often provide protections of individual rights that are even stronger than those set forth in the U.S. Constitution.

Within the guidelines of the U.S. Constitution, Congress—both the House of Representatives and the Senate—passes bills that are either vetoed or signed into law by the President. After the passage of the law, it becomes part of the United States Code, which is the official compilation of federal laws. The state legislatures use a similar process, in which bills become law when signed by the state's governor. Each state has its own official set of laws, some of which are published by the state and some of which are published by commercial publishers. The U.S. Code and the state codes are an important source of legal research; generally, legislators make efforts to make the language of the law as clear as possible.

However, reading the text of a federal or state law generally provides only part of the picture. In the American system of government, after the legislature passes laws and the executive (U.S. President or state governor) signs them, it is up to the judicial branch of the government, the court system, to interpret the laws and decide whether they violate any provision of the Constitution. At the state level, each state's supreme court has the ultimate authority in determining what a law means and whether or not it violates the state constitution. However, the federal courts—headed by the U.S. Supreme Court—can review state laws and court decisions to determine whether they violate federal laws or the U.S. Constitution. For example, a state court may find that a particular criminal law is valid under the state's constitution, but a federal court may then review the state court's decision and determine that the law is invalid under the U.S. Constitution.

It is important, then, to read court decisions when doing legal research. The Constitution uses language that is intentionally very general—for example, prohibiting "unreasonable searches and seizures" by the police—and court cases often provide more guidance. For example, the U.S. Supreme Court's 2001 decision in *Kyllo* v. *United States* held that scanning the outside of a person's house using a heat sensor to determine whether the person is growing marijuana is unreasonable—*if* it is done without a search warrant secured from a judge. Supreme Court decisions provide the most definitive explanation of the law of the land, and it is therefore important to include these in research. Often, when the Supreme Court has not decided a case on a particular issue, a decision by a federal appeals court or a state supreme court can provide guidance; but just as laws and constitutions can vary from state to state, so can federal courts be split on a particular interpretation of federal law or the U.S. Constitution. For example, federal appeals courts in Louisiana and California may reach opposite conclusions in similar cases.

Lawyers and courts refer to statutes and court decisions through a formal system of citations. Use of these citations reveals which court made the decision (or which legislature passed the statute) and when and enables the reader to locate the statute or court case quickly in a law library. For example, the legendary Supreme Court case *Brown* v. *Board of Education* has the legal citation 347 U.S. 483 (1954). At a law library, this 1954 decision can be found on page 483 of volume 347 of the U.S. Reports, the official collection of the Supreme Court's decisions. Citations can also be helpful in locating court cases on the Internet.

Understanding the current state of the law leads only to a partial understanding of the issues covered by the POINT/COUNTERPOINT series. For a fuller understanding of the issues, it is necessary to look at public-policy arguments that the current state of the law is not adequately addressing the issue.

Many groups lobby for new legislation or changes to existing legislation; the National Rifle Association (NRA), for example, lobbies Congress and the state legislatures constantly to make existing gun control laws less restrictive and not to pass additional laws. The NRA and other groups dedicated to various causes might also intervene in pending court cases: a group such as Planned Parenthood might file a brief *amicus curiae* (as "a friend of the court")—called an "amicus brief"—in a lawsuit that could affect abortion rights. Interest groups also use the media to influence public opinion, issuing press releases and frequently appearing in interviews on news programs and talk shows. The books in POINT/COUNTERPOINT list some of the interest groups that are active in the issue at hand, but in each case there are countless other groups working at the local, state, and national levels. It is important to read everything with a critical eye, for sometimes interest groups present information in a way that can be read only to their advantage. The informed reader must always look for bias.

Finding sources of legal information on the Internet is relatively simple thanks to "portal" sites such as FindLaw (*www.findlaw.com*), which provides access to a variety of constitutions, statutes, court opinions, law review articles, news articles, and other resources—including all Supreme Court decisions issued since 1893. Other useful sources of information include the U.S. Government Printing Office (*www.gpo.gov*), which contains a complete copy of the U.S. Code, and the Library of Congress's THOMAS system (*thomas.loc.gov*), which offers access to bills pending before Congress as well as recently passed laws. Of course, the Internet changes every second of every day, so it is best to do some independent searching. Most cases, studies, and opinions that are cited or referred to in public debate can be found online—and *everything* can be found in one library or another.

The Internet can provide a basic understanding of most important legal issues, but not all sources can be found there. To find some documents it is necessary to visit the law library of a university or a public law library; some cities have public law libraries, and many library systems keep legal documents at the main branch. On the following page are some common citation forms.

Source of Law	Sample Citation	Notes
U.S. Supreme Court	*Employment Division* v. *Smith*, 485 U.S. 660 (1988)	The U.S. Reports is the official record of Supreme Court decisions. There is also an unofficial Supreme Court ("S. Ct.") reporter.
U.S. Court of Appeals	*United States* v. *Lambert*, 695 F.2d 536 (11th Cir.1983)	Appellate cases appear in the Federal Reporter, designated by "F." The 11th Circuit has jurisdiction in Alabama, Florida, and Georgia.
U.S. District Court	*Carillon Importers, Ltd.* v. *Frank Pesce Group, Inc.*, 913 F.Supp. 1559 (S.D.Fla.1996)	Federal trial-level decisions are reported in the Federal Supplement ("F. Supp."). Some states have multiple federal districts; this case originated in the Southern District of Florida.
U.S. Code	Thomas Jefferson Commemoration Commission Act, 36 U.S.C., §149 (2002)	Sometimes the popular names of legislation—names with which the public may be familiar—are included with the U.S. Code citation.
State Supreme Court	*Sterling* v. *Cupp*, 290 Ore. 611, 614, 625 P.2d 123, 126 (1981)	The Oregon Supreme Court decision is reported in both the state's reporter and the Pacific regional reporter.
State Statute	Pennsylvania Abortion Control Act of 1982, 18 Pa. Cons. Stat. 3203-3220 (1990)	States use many different citation formats for their statutes.

103

PICTURE CREDITS ///|||//

CONTRIBUTORS

DAVID L. HUDSON, JR., is an author-attorney who has published widely on First Amendment and other constitutional law issues. Hudson is a research attorney with the First Amendment Center at Vanderbilt University and a First Amendment contributing editor to the American Bar Association's *Preview of the United States Supreme Court Cases*. He obtained his undergraduate degree from Duke University and his law degree from Vanderbilt University Law School.

ALAN MARZILLI, M.A., J.D., lives in Washington, D.C., and is a program associate with Advocates for Human Potential, Inc., a research and consulting firm based in Sudbury, Mass., and Albany, N.Y. He primarily works on developing training and educational materials for agencies of the federal government on topics such as housing, mental health policy, employment, and transportation. He has spoken on mental health issues in 30 states, the District of Columbia, and Puerto Rico; his work has included training mental health administrators, nonprofit management and staff, and people with mental illnesses and their families on a wide variety of topics, including effective advocacy, community-based mental health services, and housing. He has written several handbooks and training curricula that are used nationally and as far away as the territory of Guam. He managed statewide and national mental health advocacy programs and worked for several public interest lobbying organizations while studying law at Georgetown University. He has written more than a dozen books, including numerous titles in the *Point/Counterpoint* series.